Photography Portfolio

Decades of being around accomplished talent producing absolutely phenomenal quality work has taught that we are capable of greatness. It is possible to meet our destiny and become it. Experiencing excellence done with such apparent ease and humble selfless gratification is the motivation for this photography. Most important was having the freedom

Being colorblind gives an advantage when composing black & white… less confusion. This special collection selected from thousands of captures. All images were framed in the camera and presented without edits, genuine as seen through the lens. RAW conversion applied by proprietary panchromatic process from source files.

Limited edition fine art and custom work available.

info@ BEACHNOISE.com

Joseph Fleming

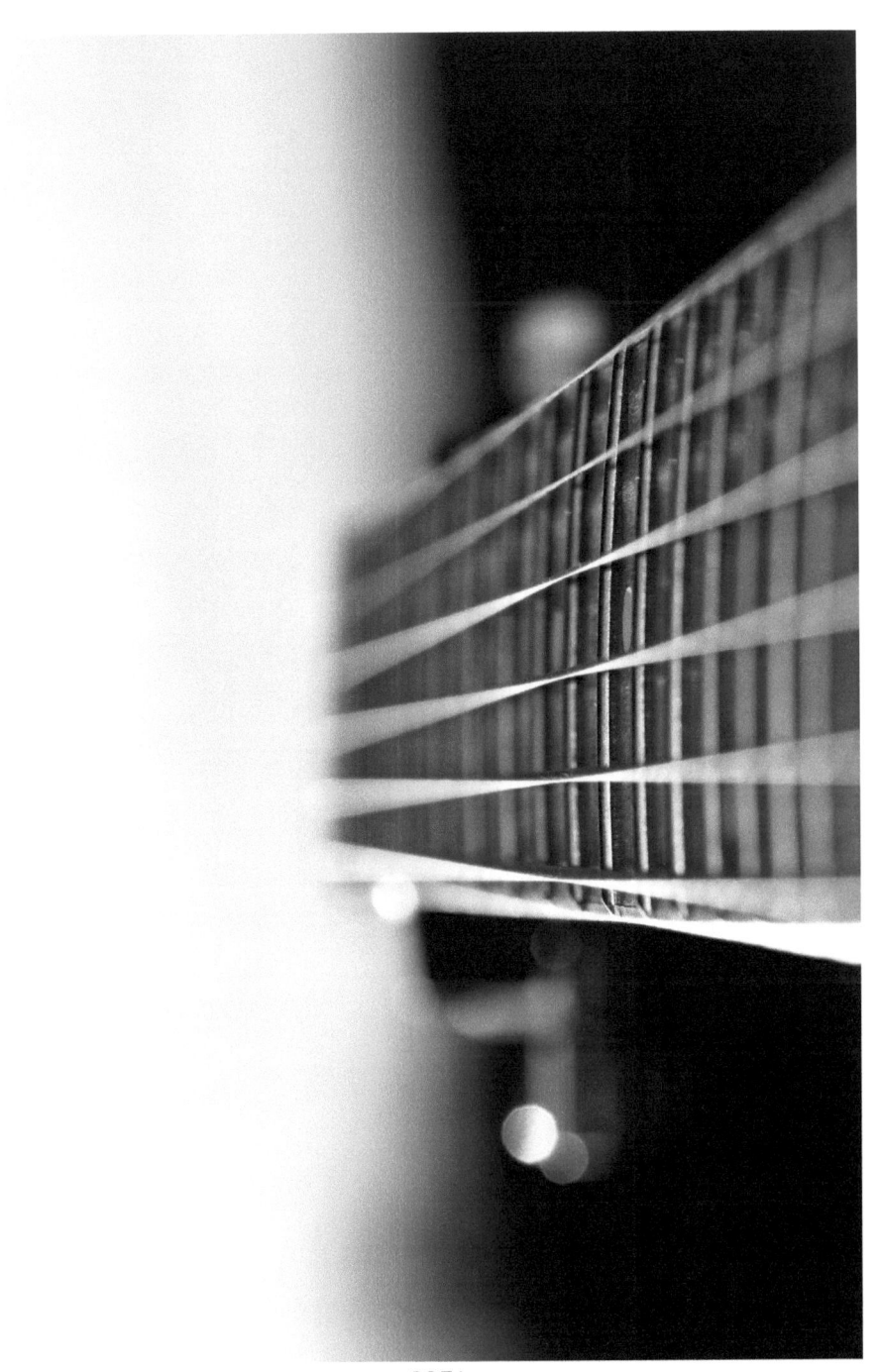

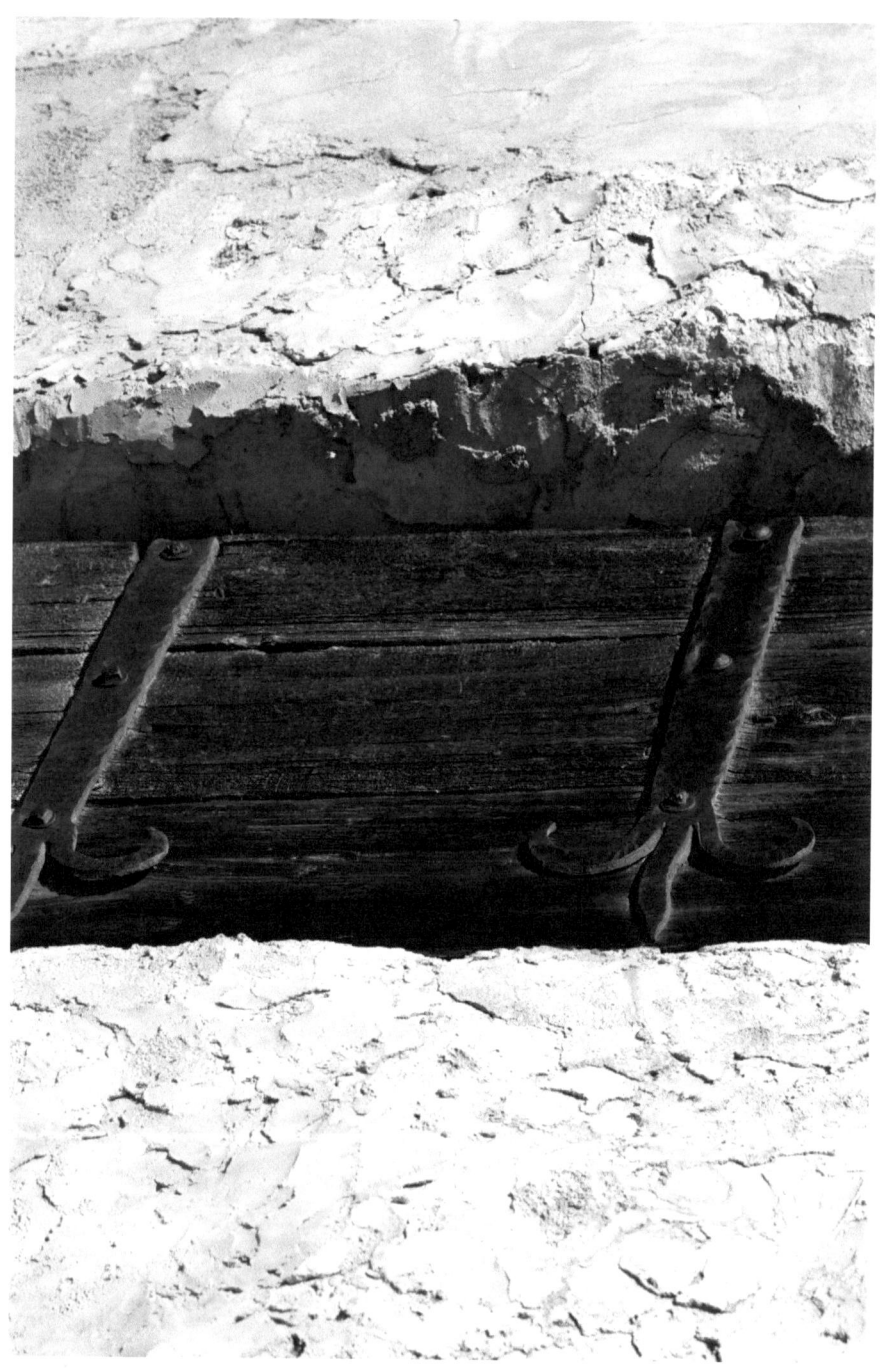

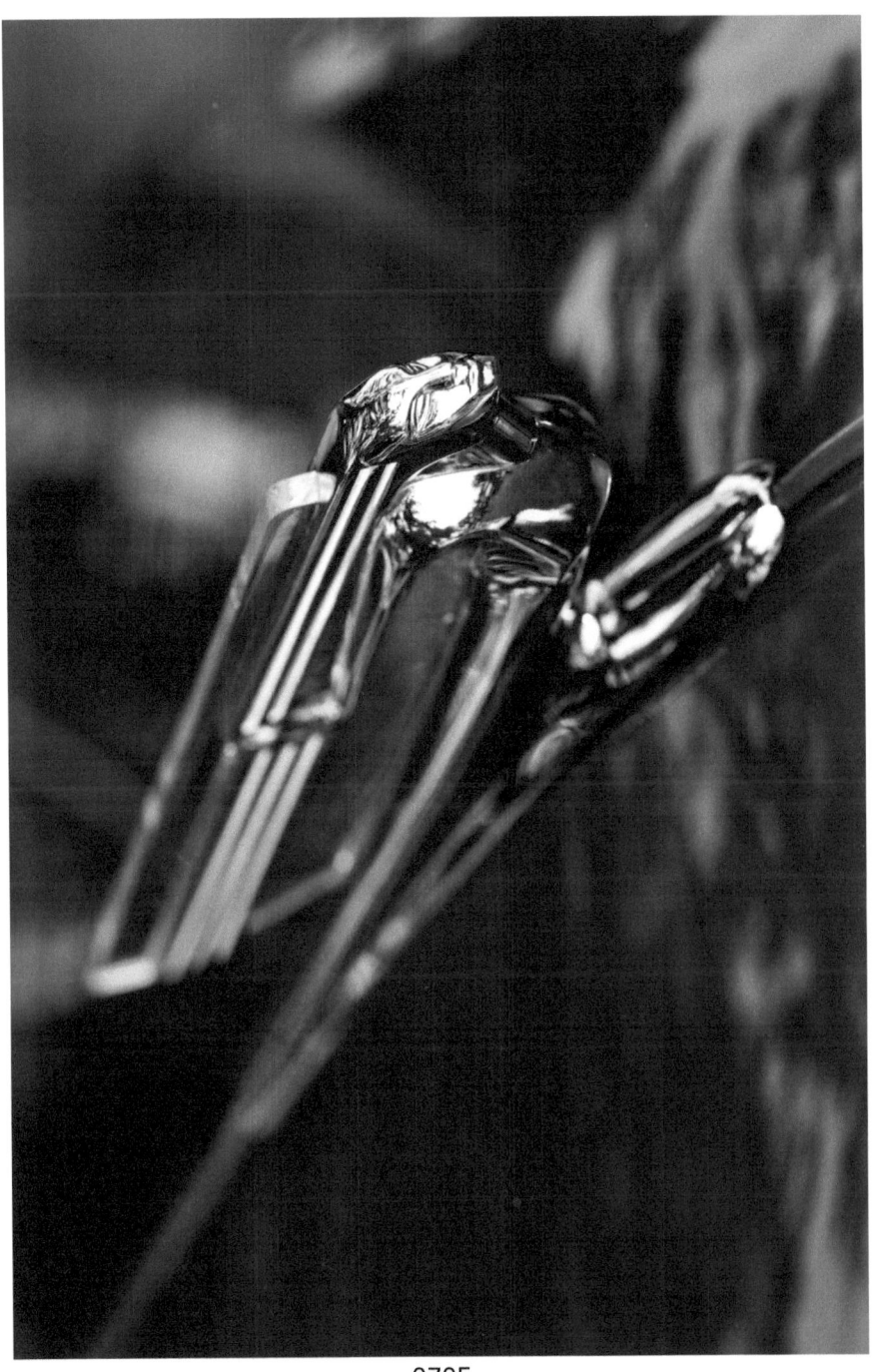

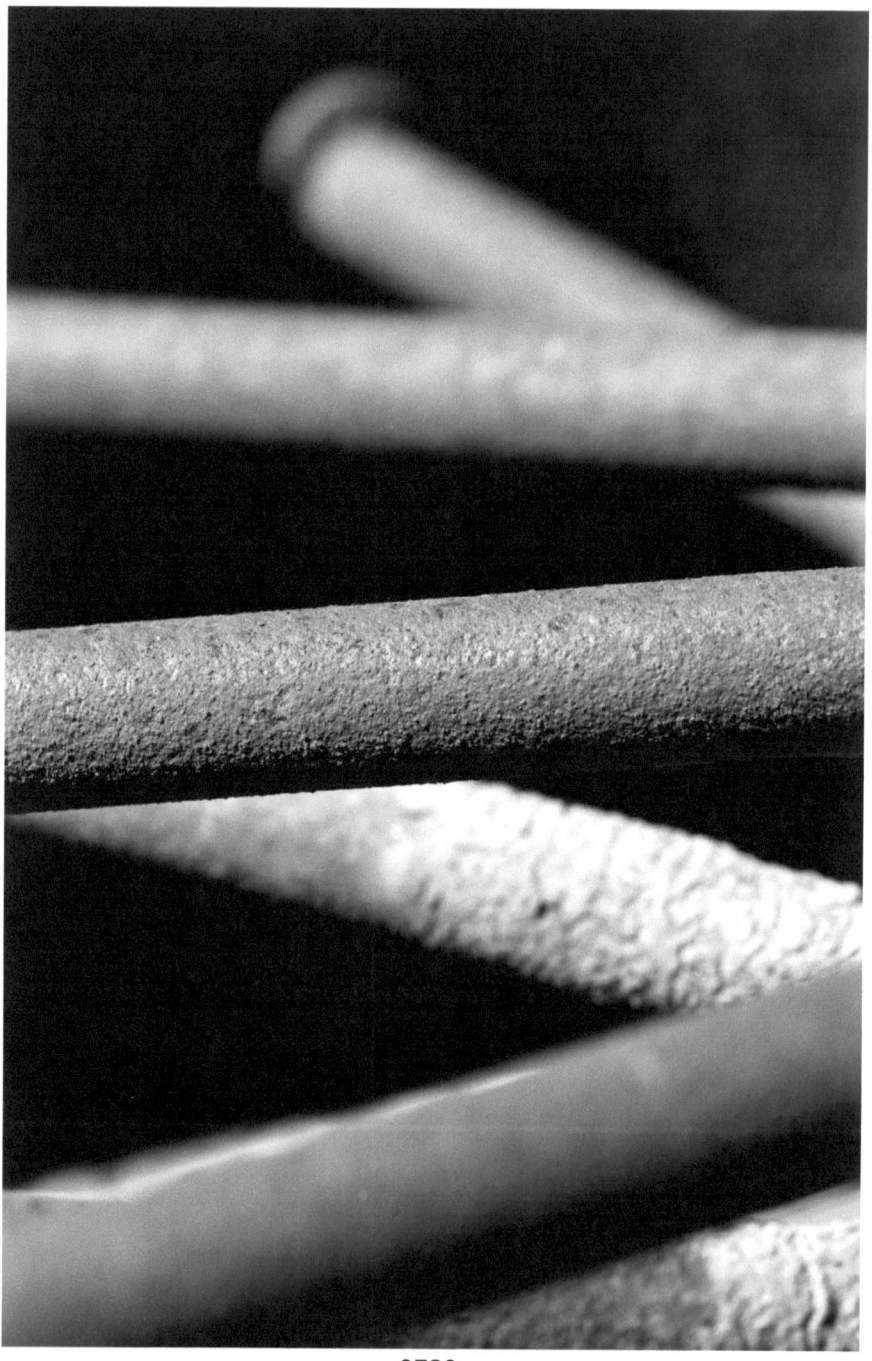

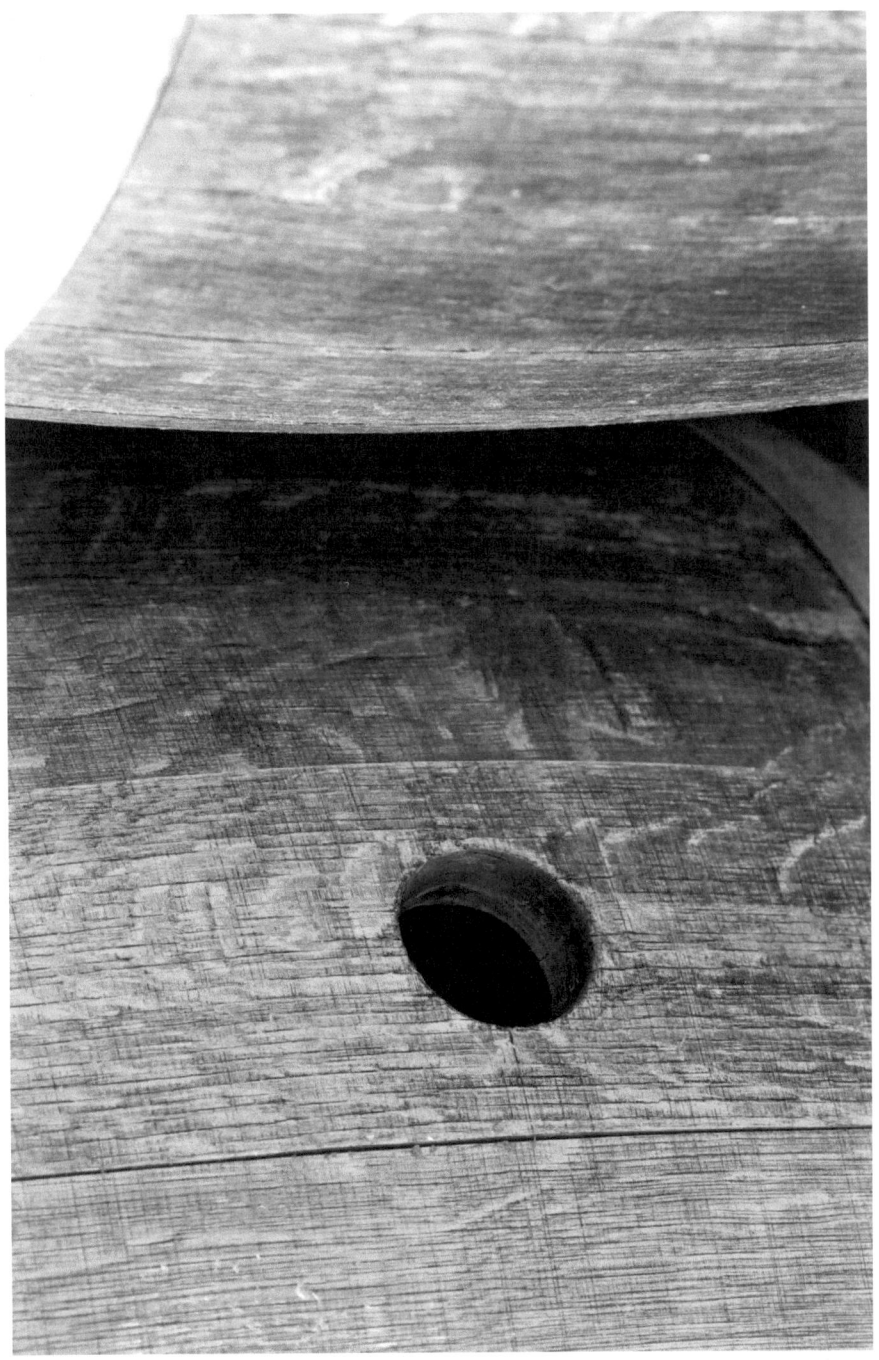

0826

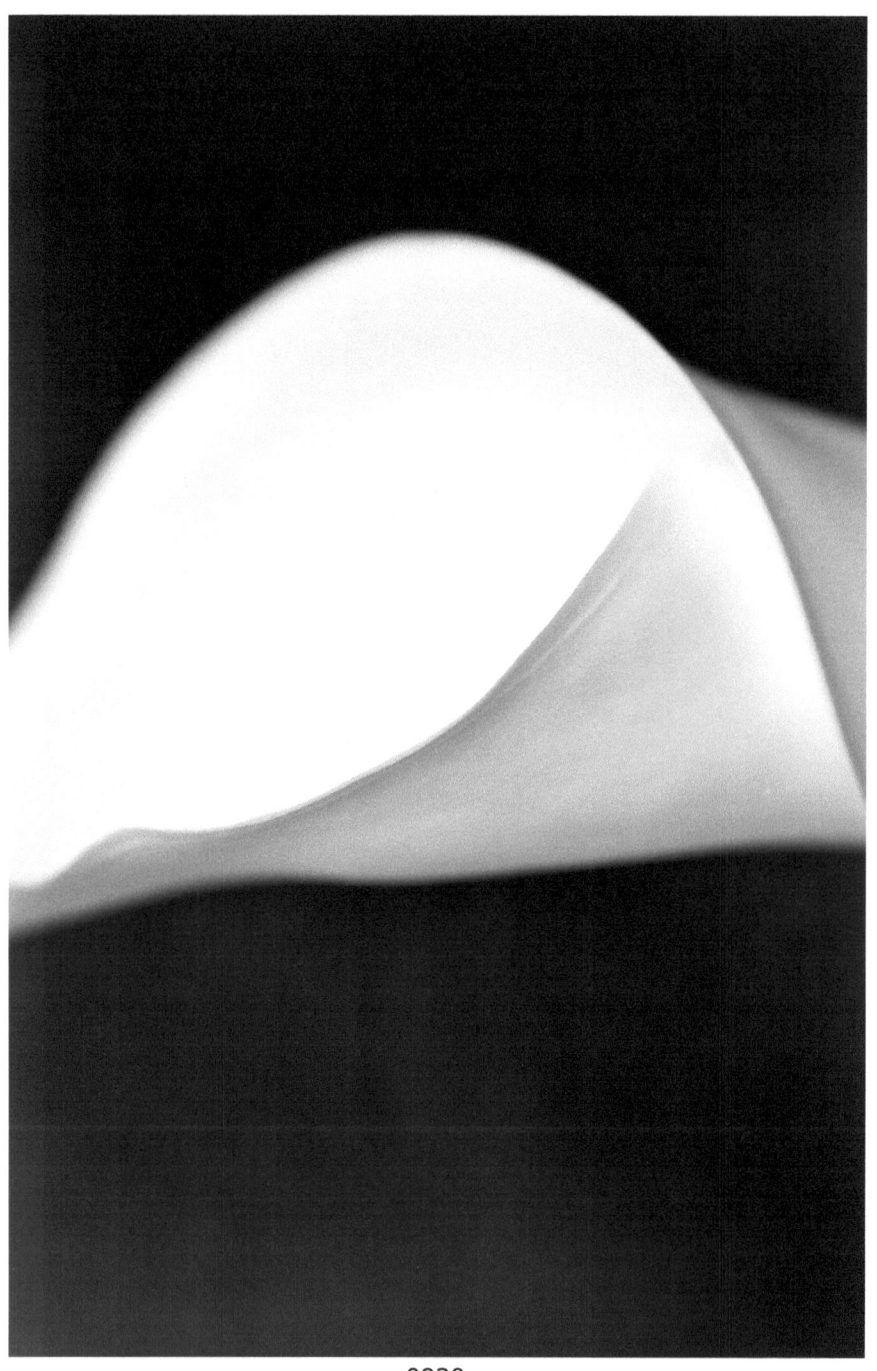

0920

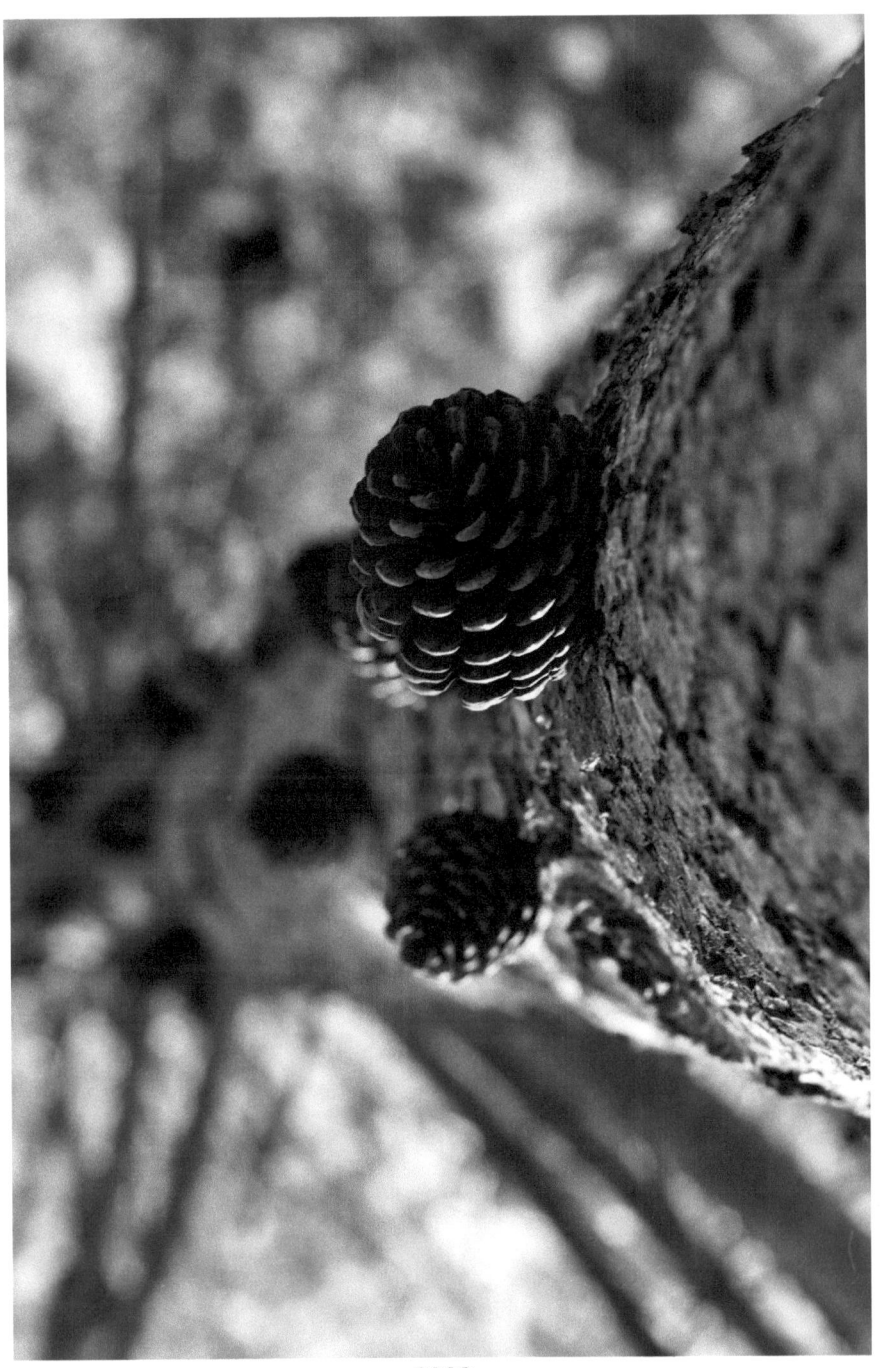

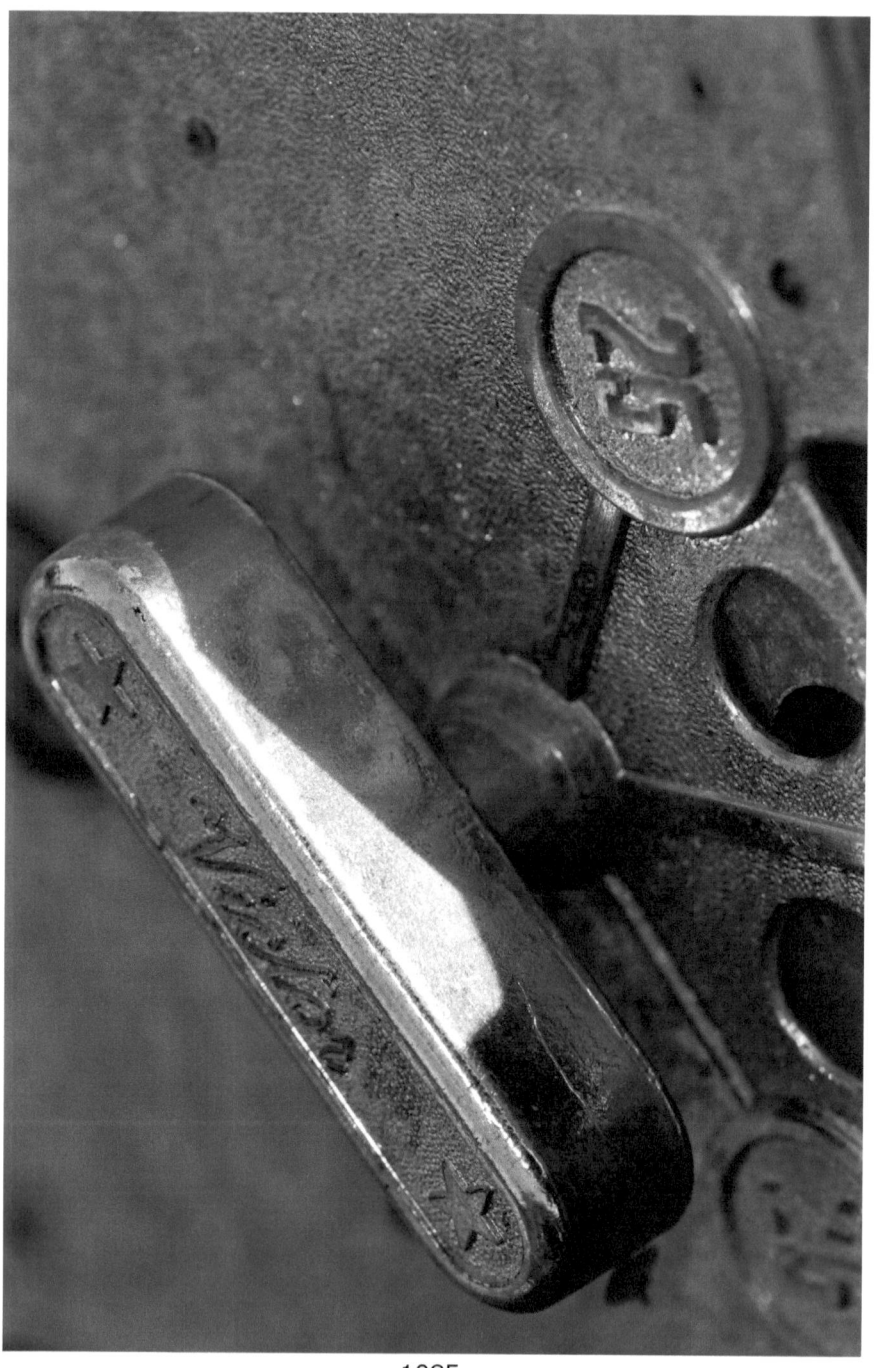

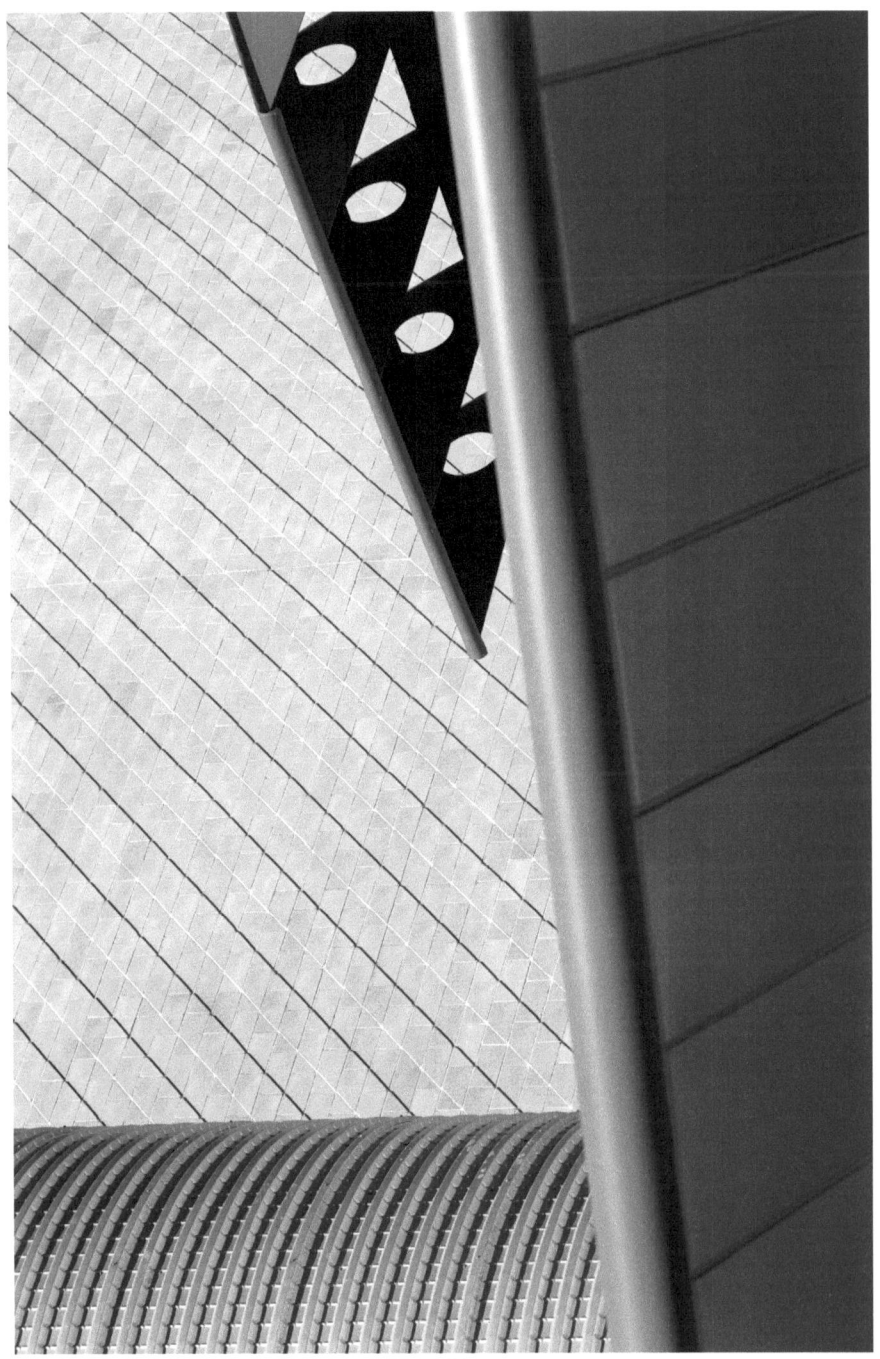

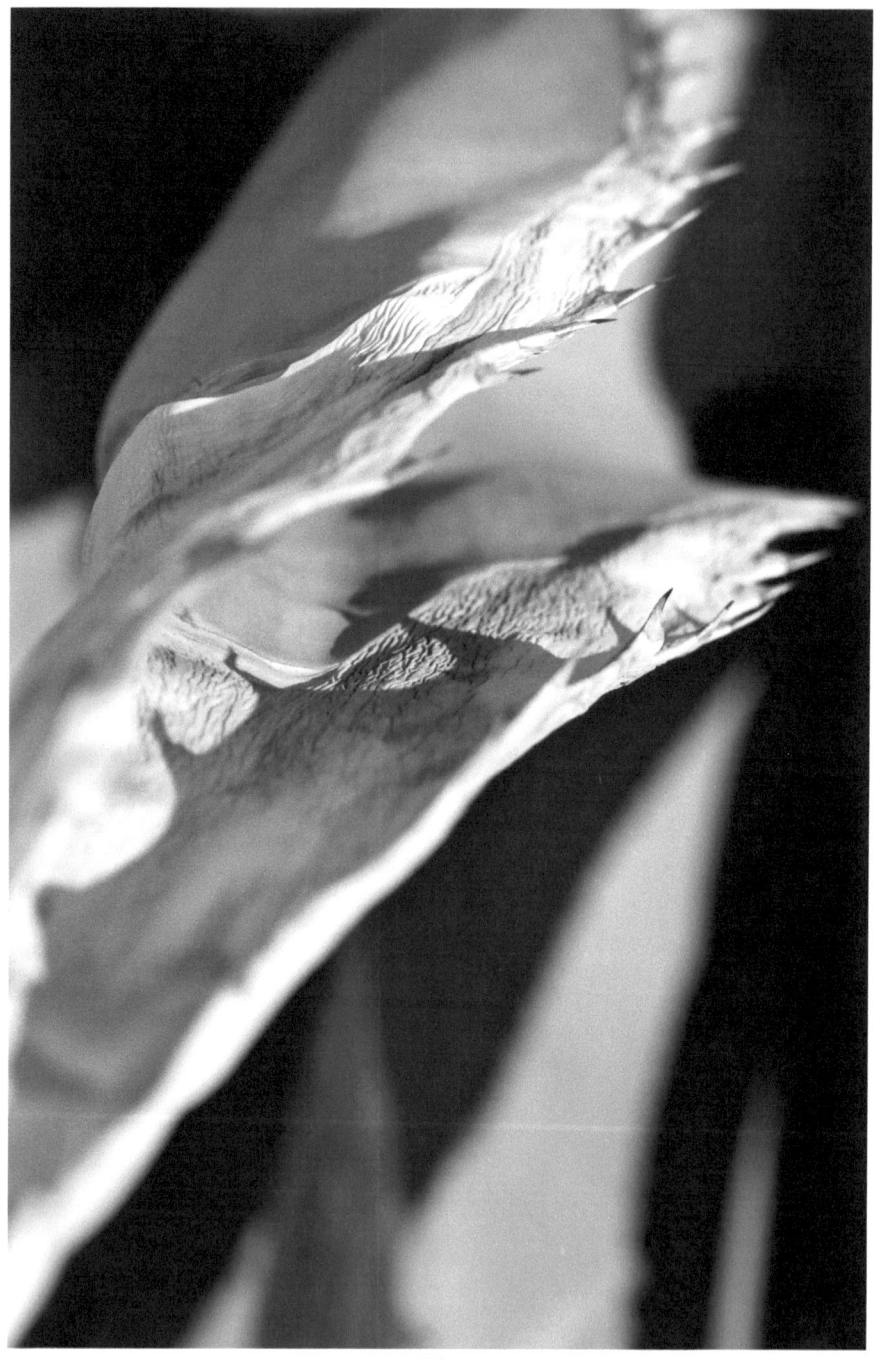

1581

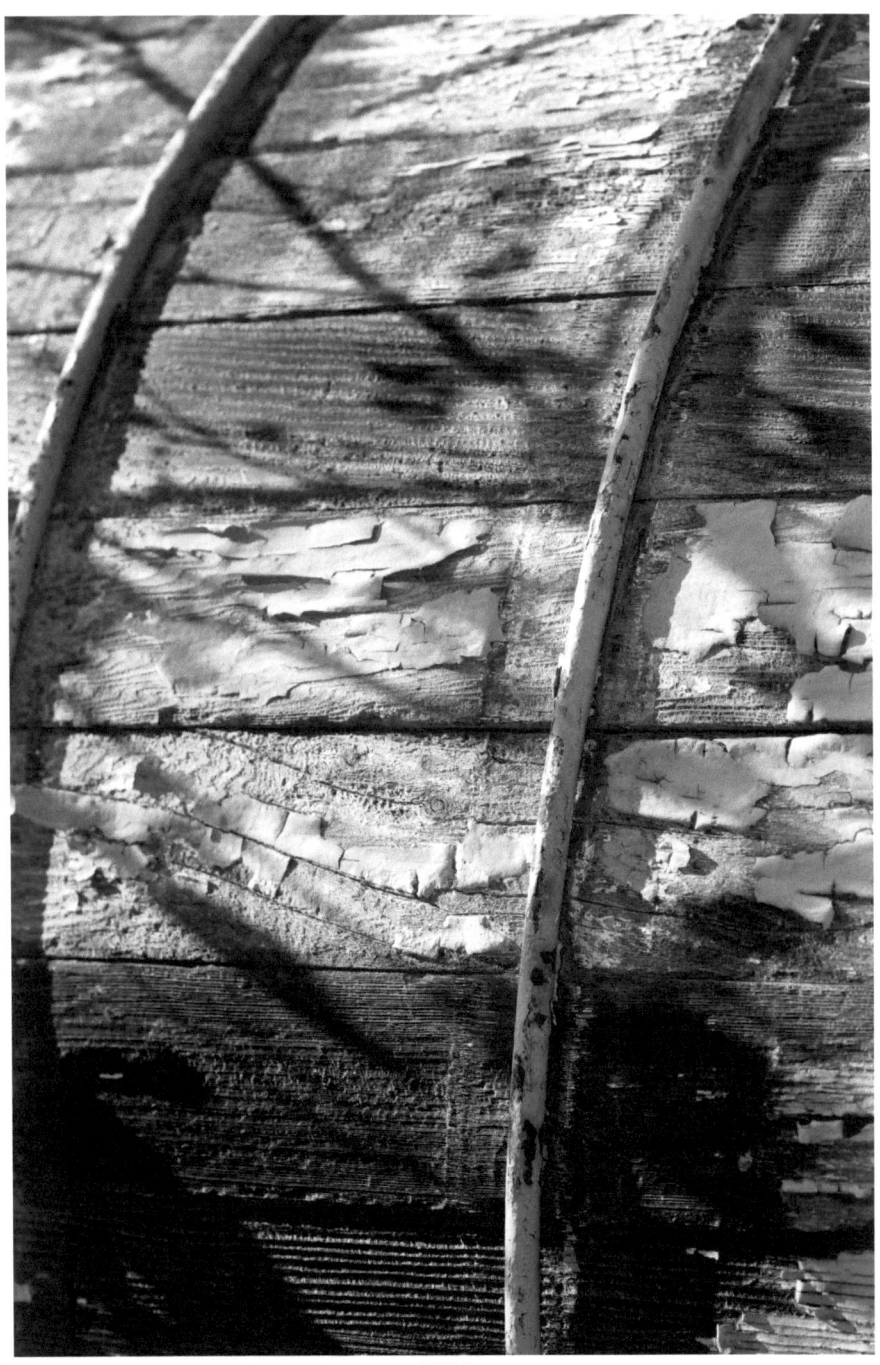

1608

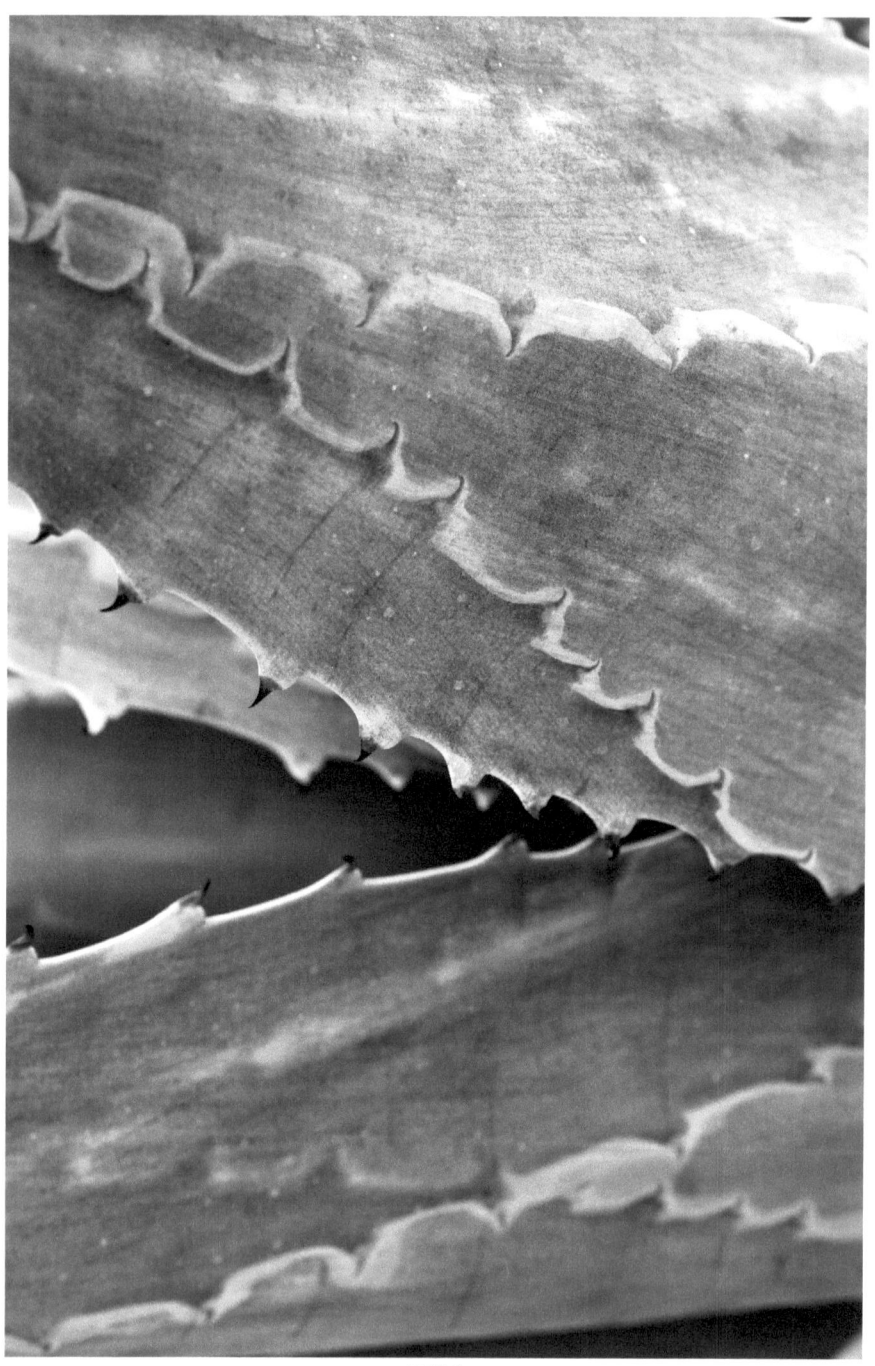

1976

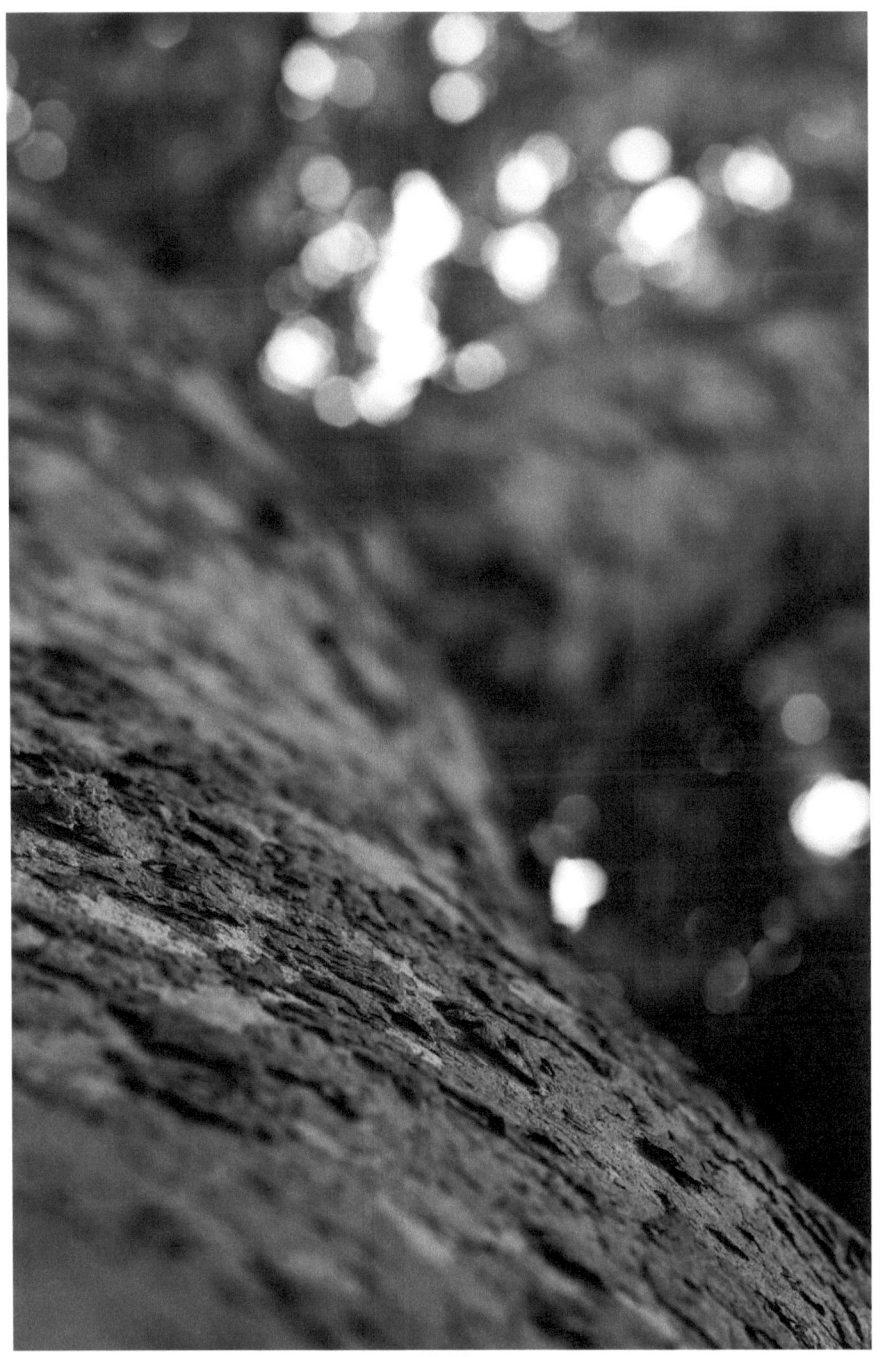

2068

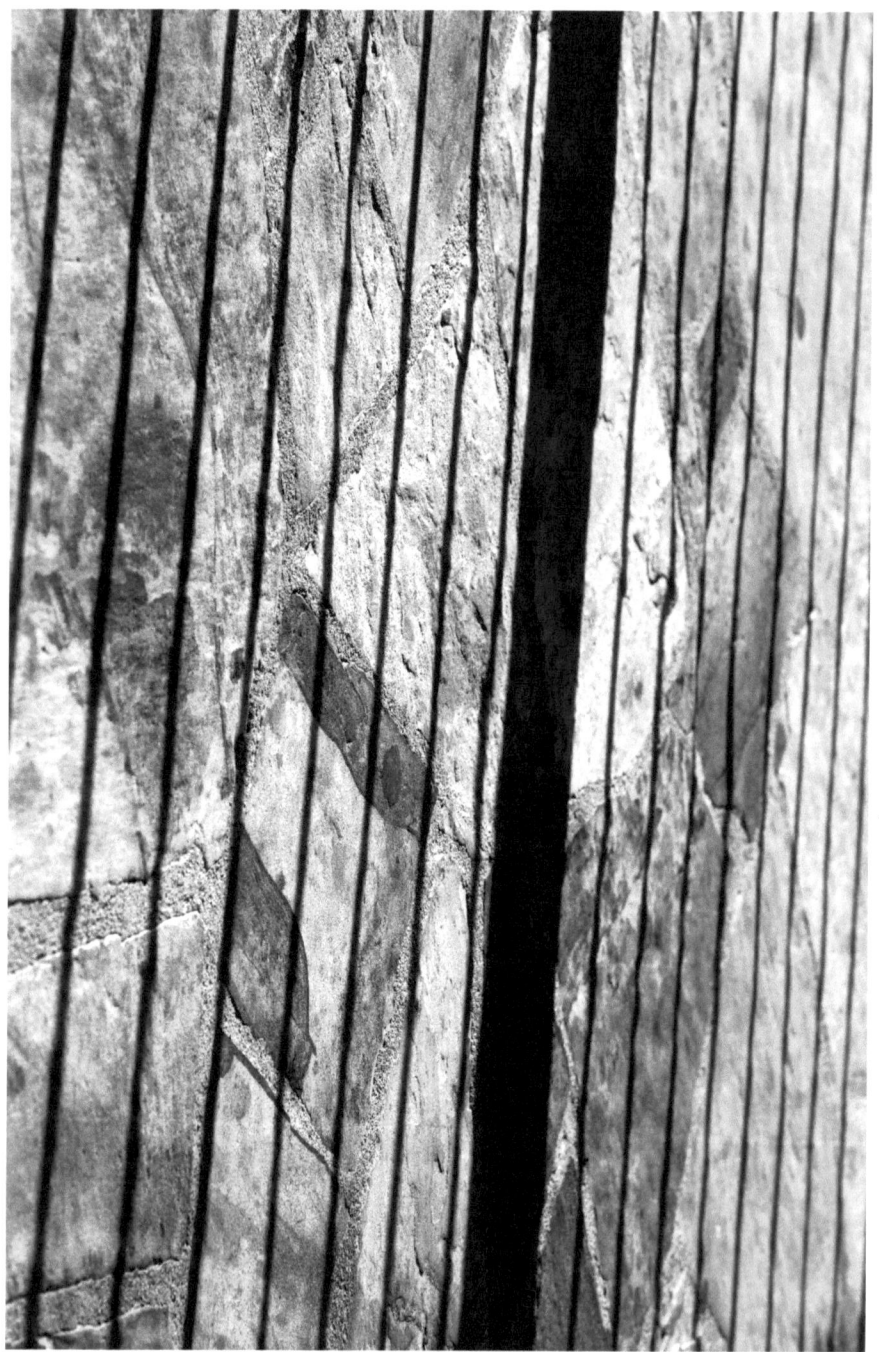

2089

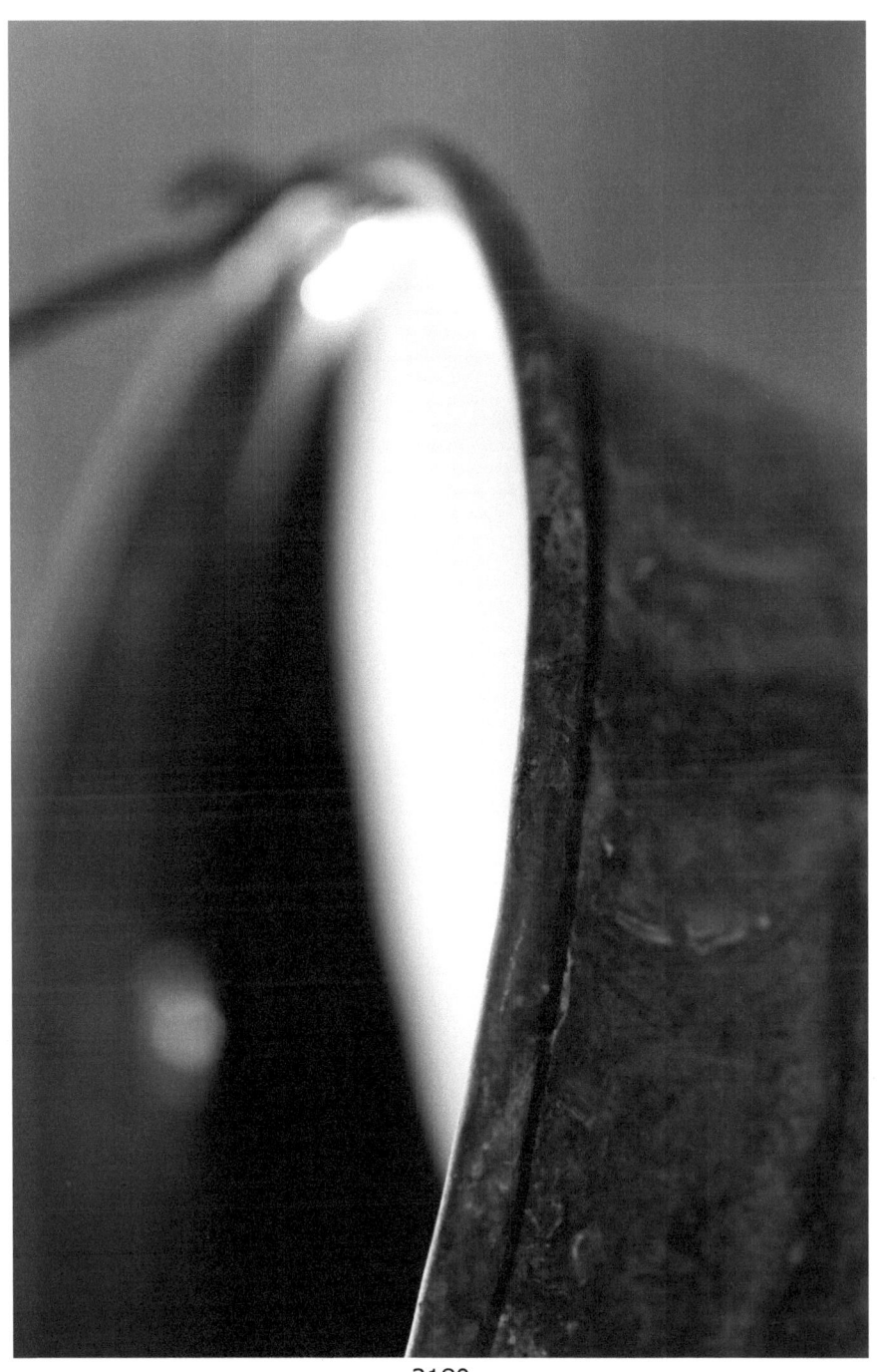

2180

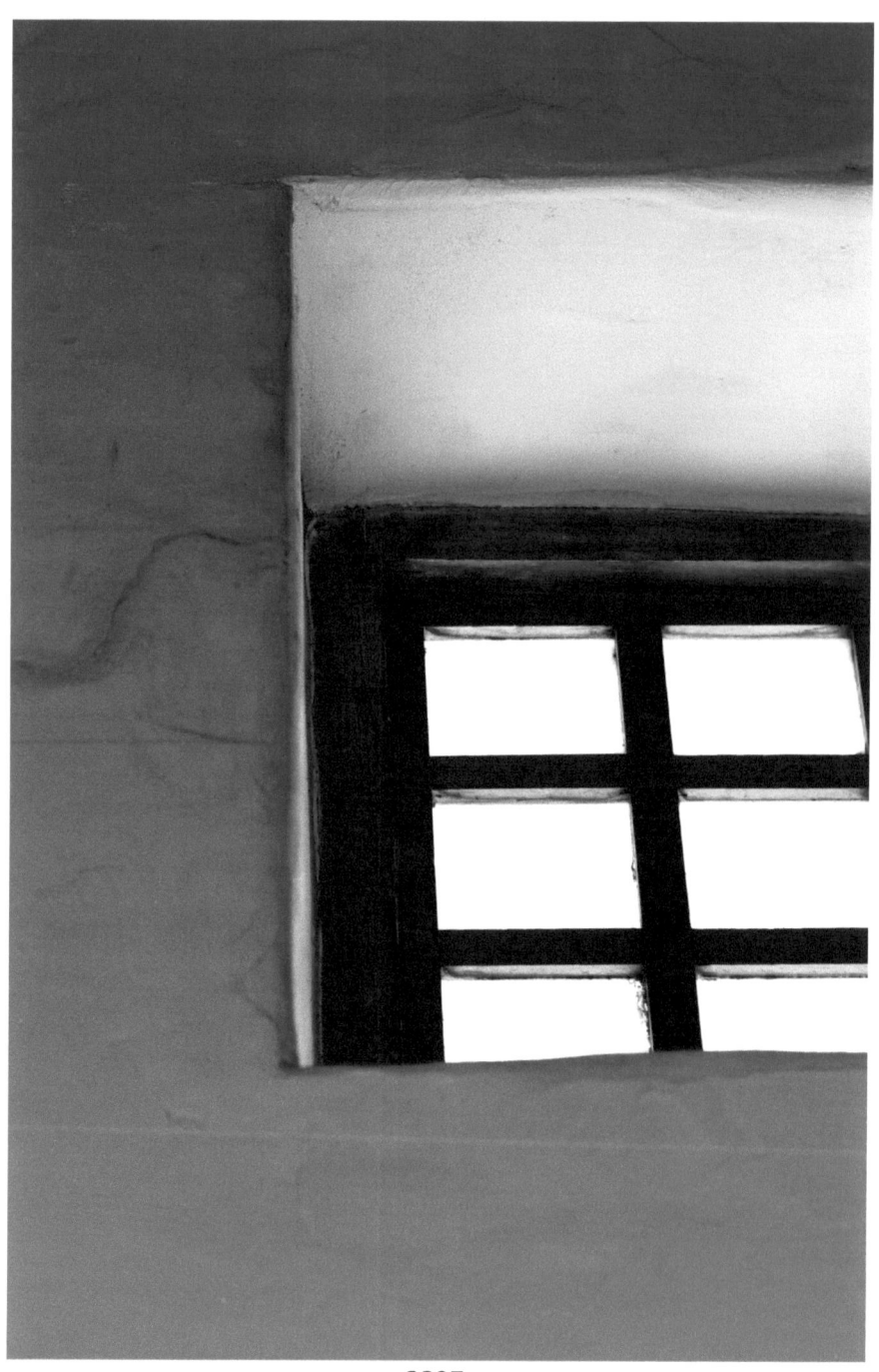

2397

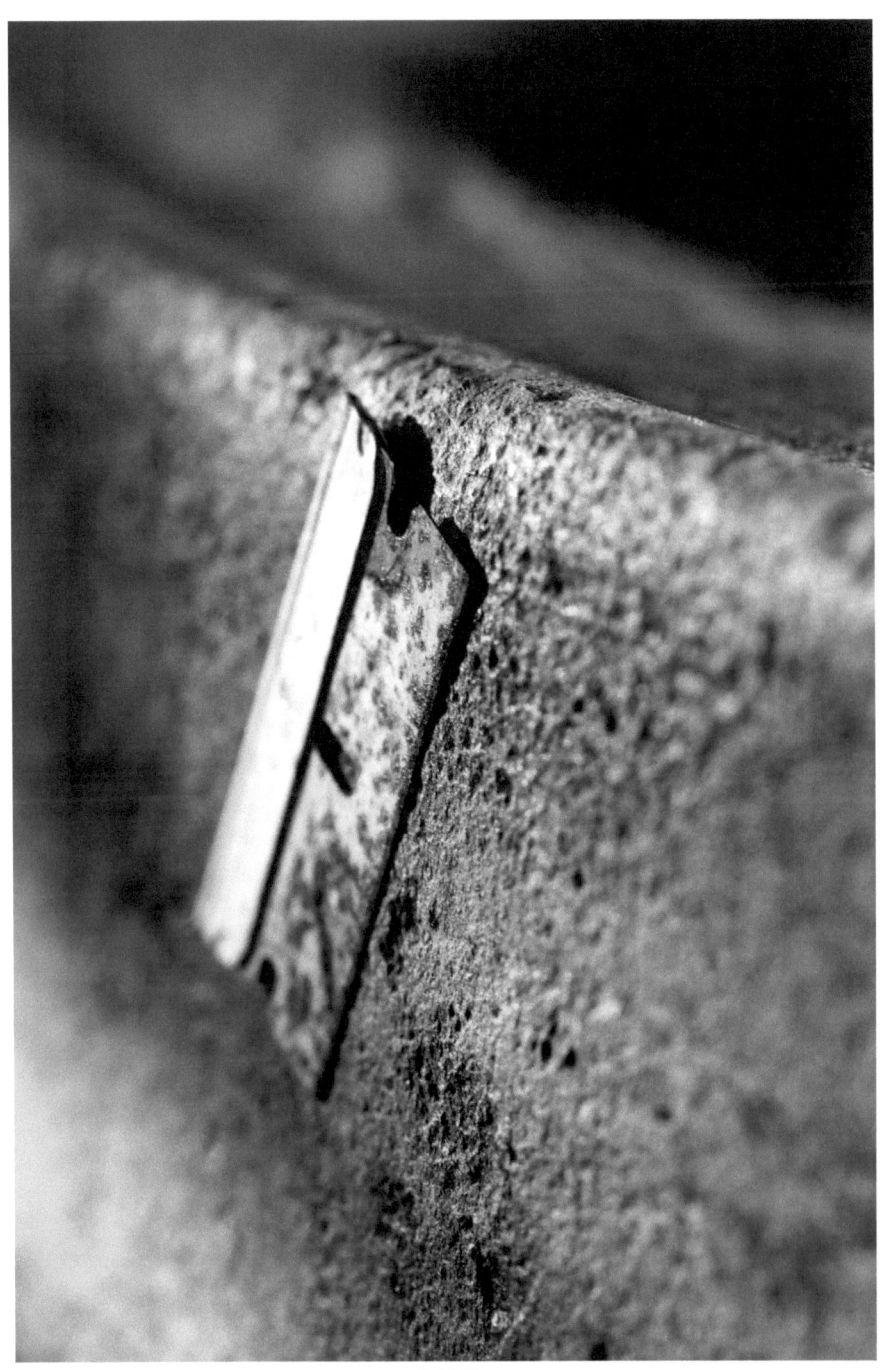

2467

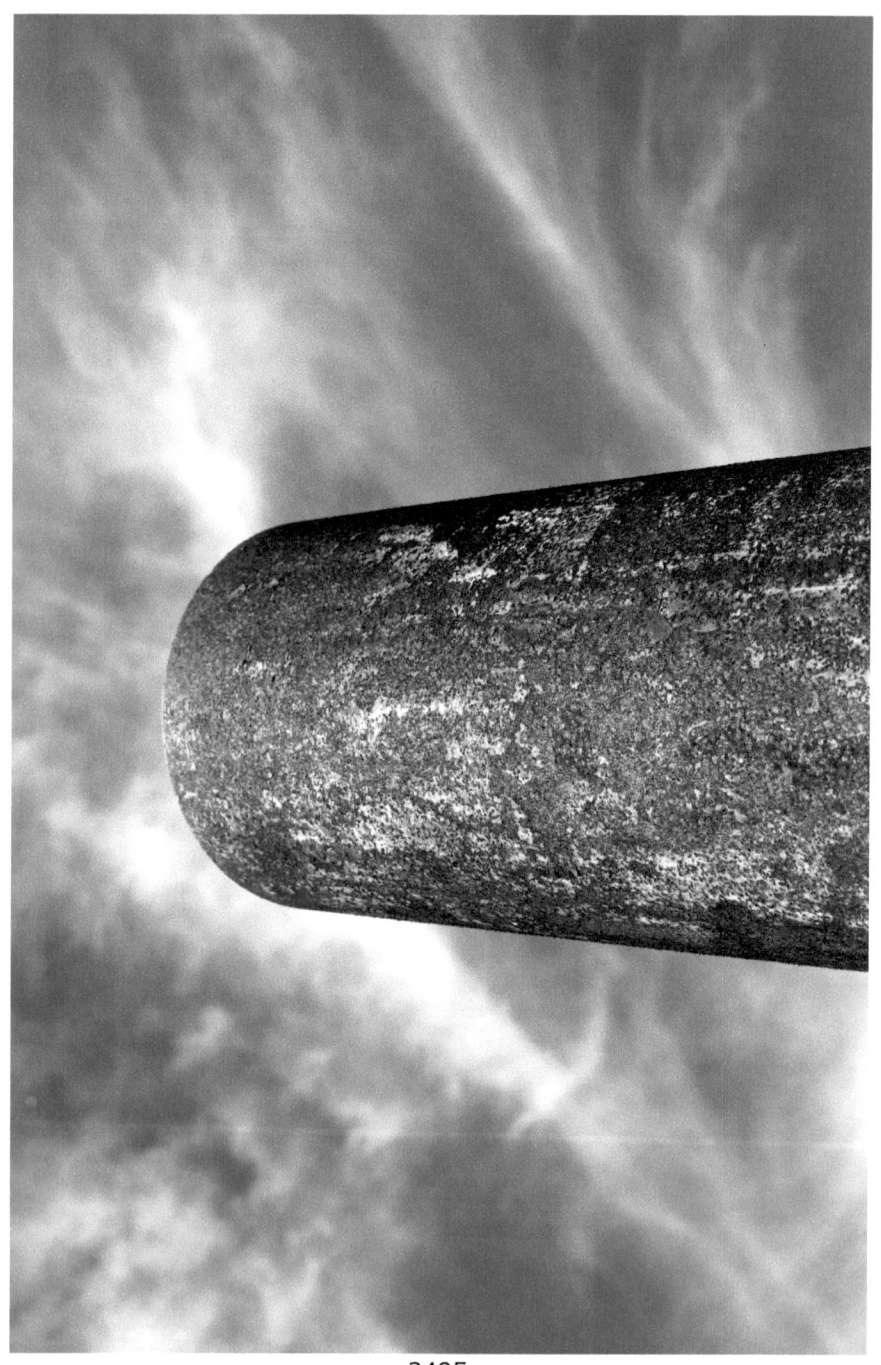

2495

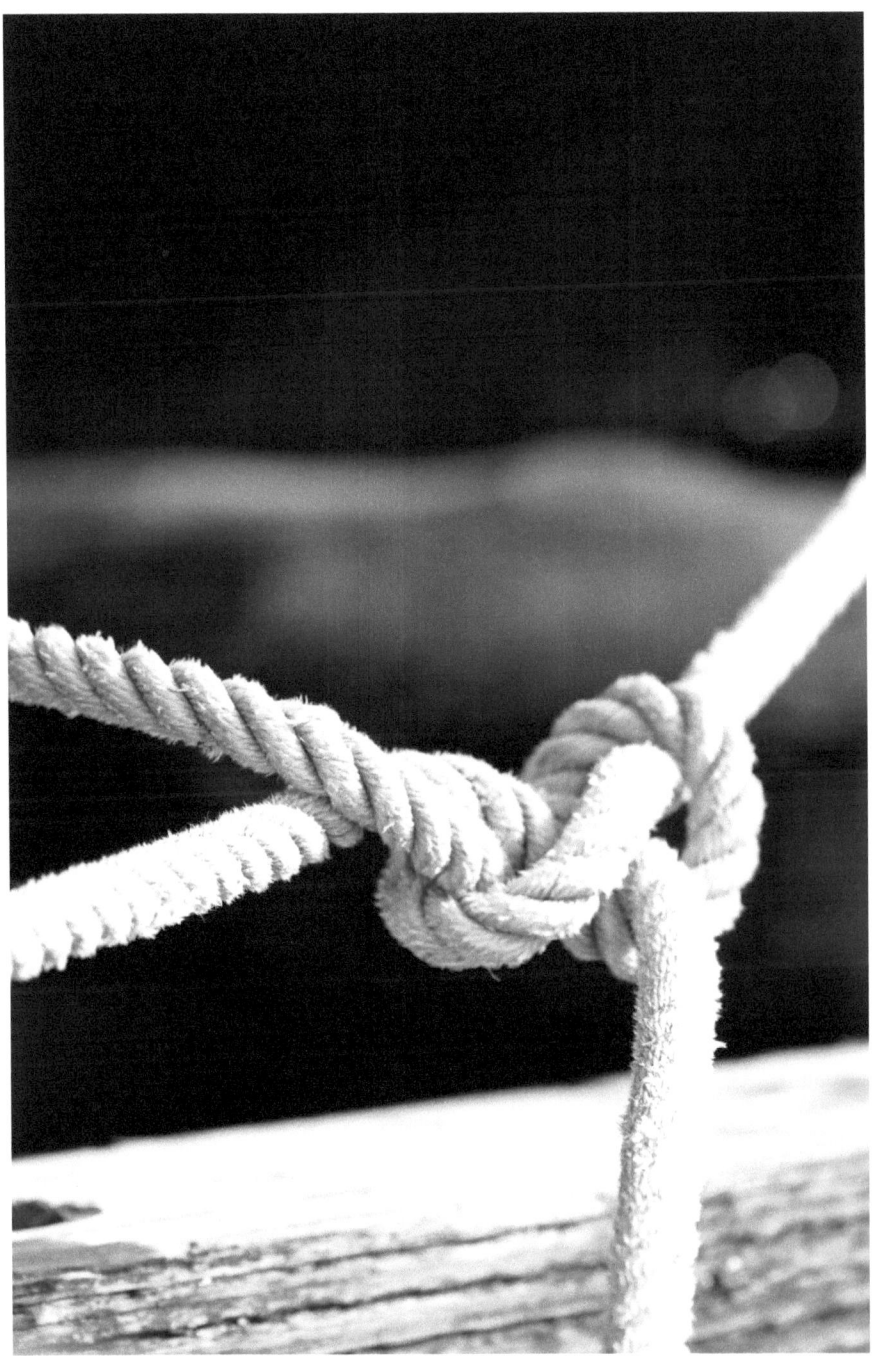

2686

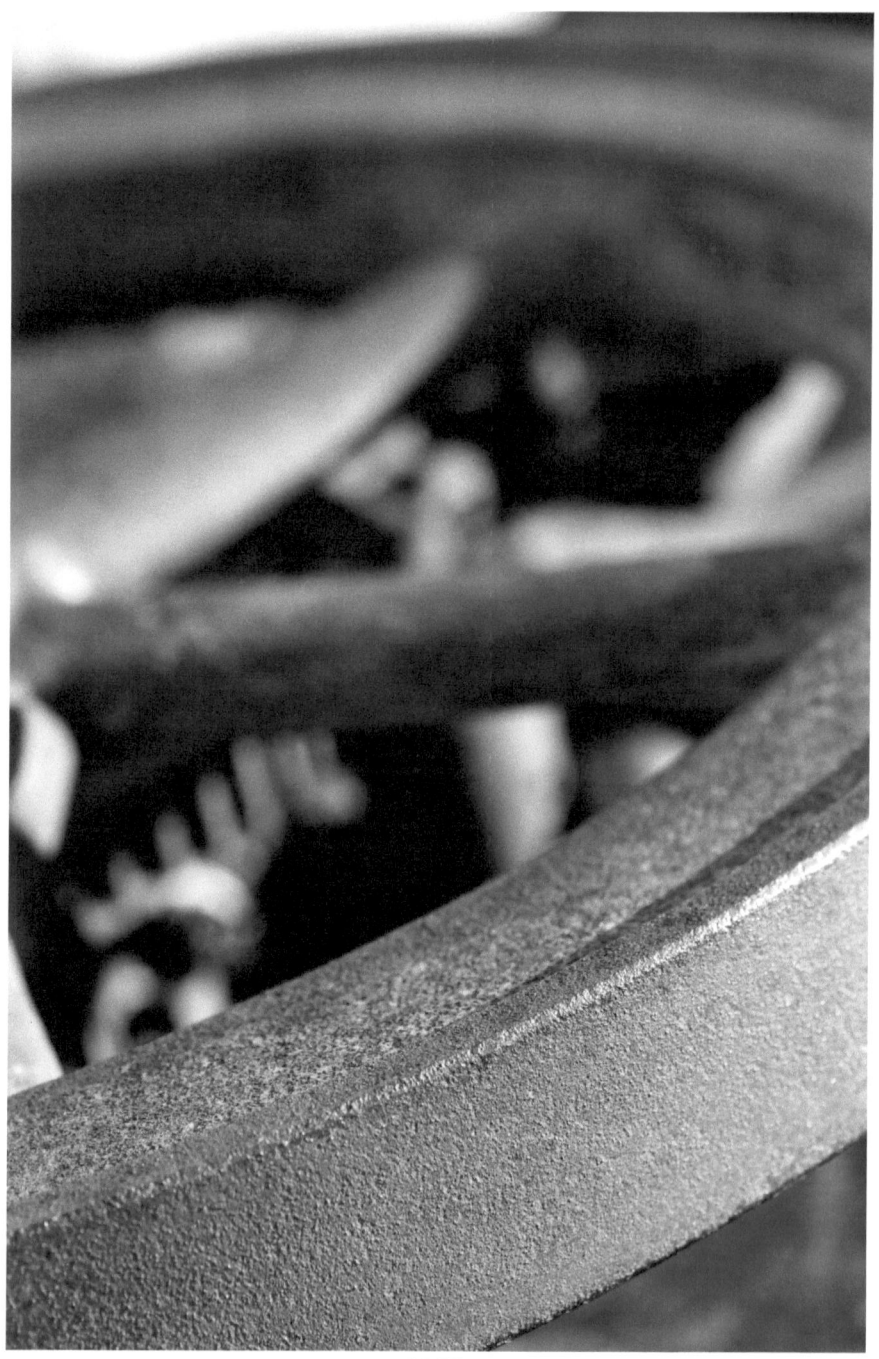

2962

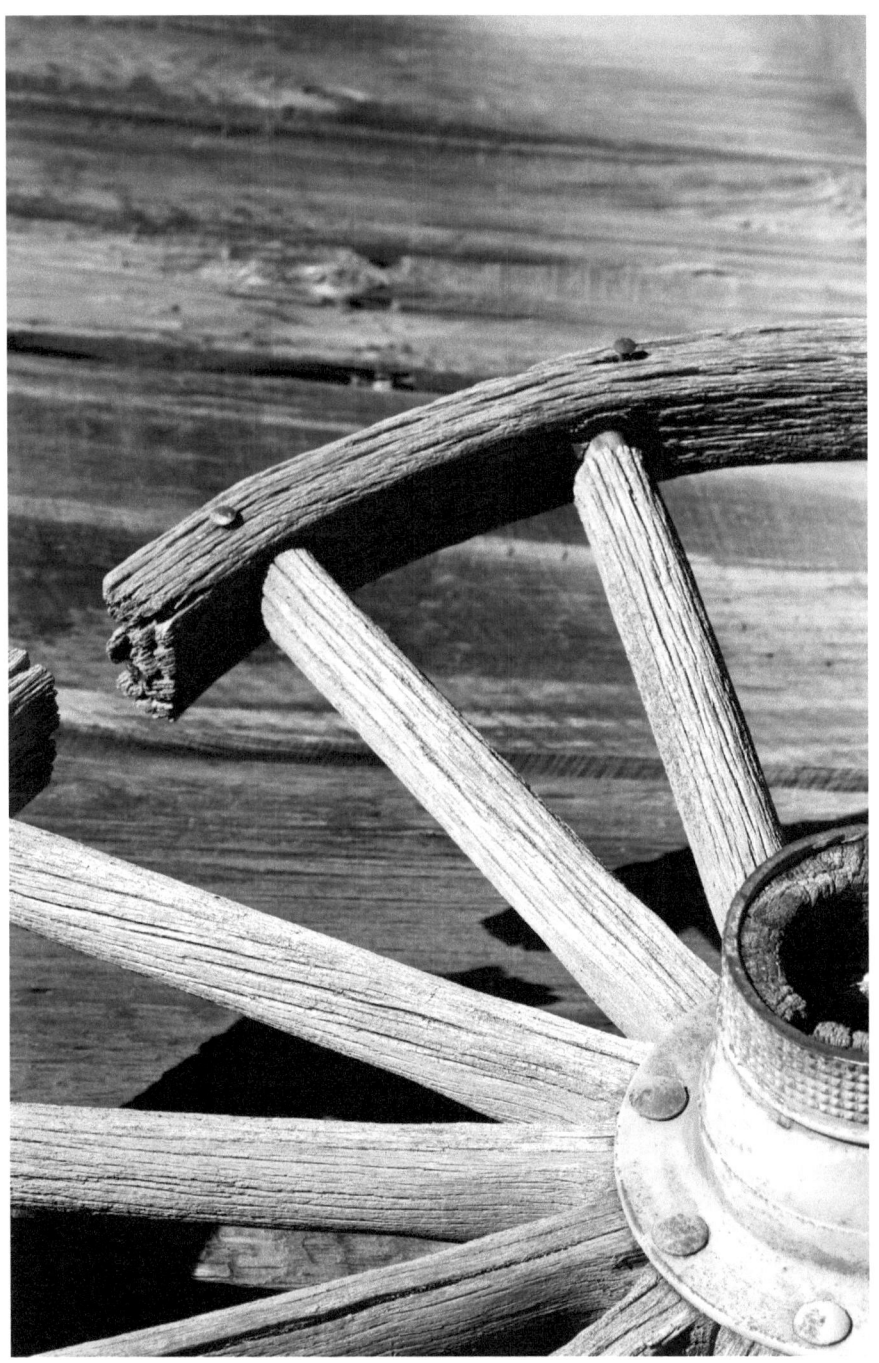

3147

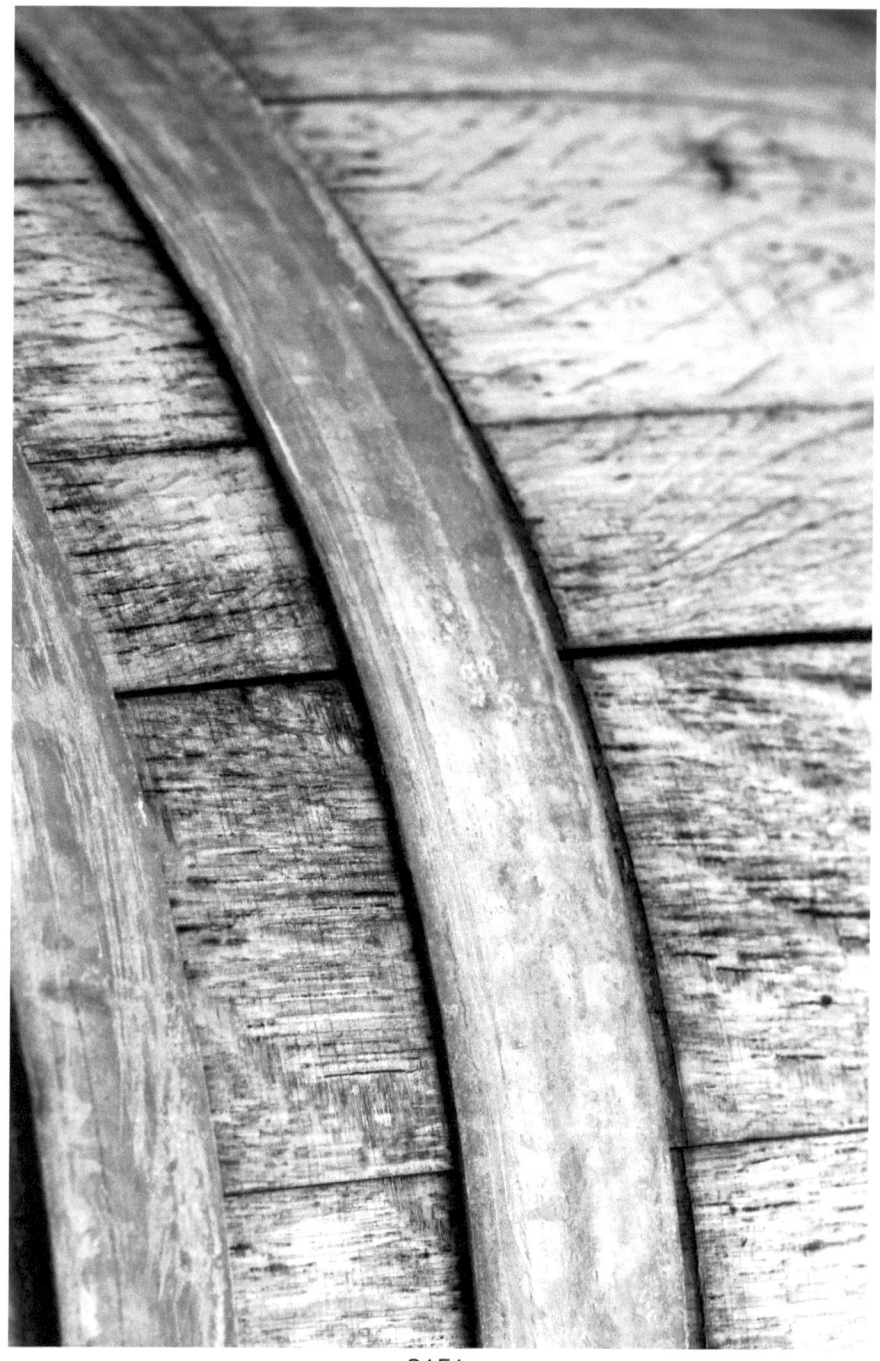

3151

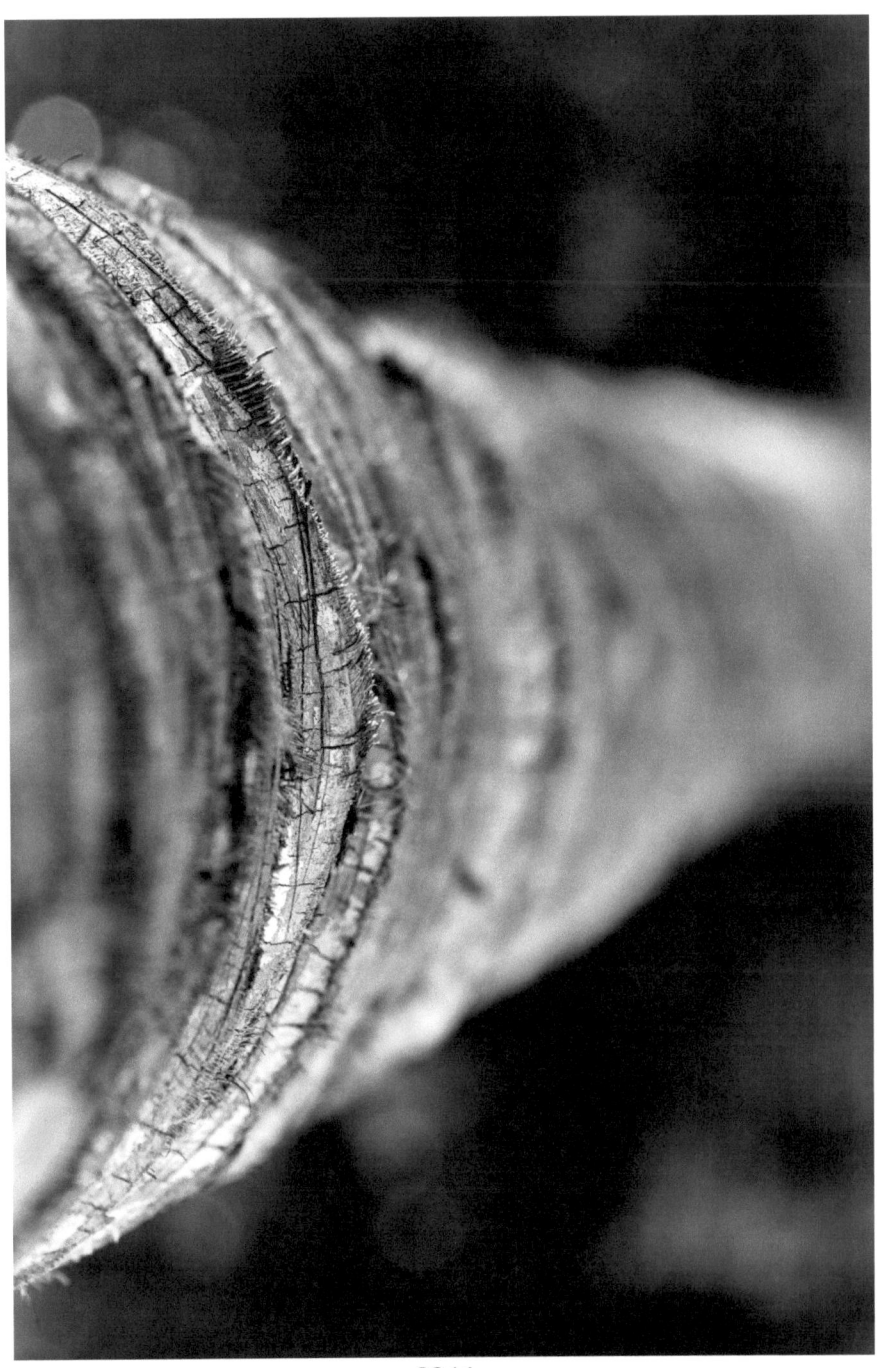

3244

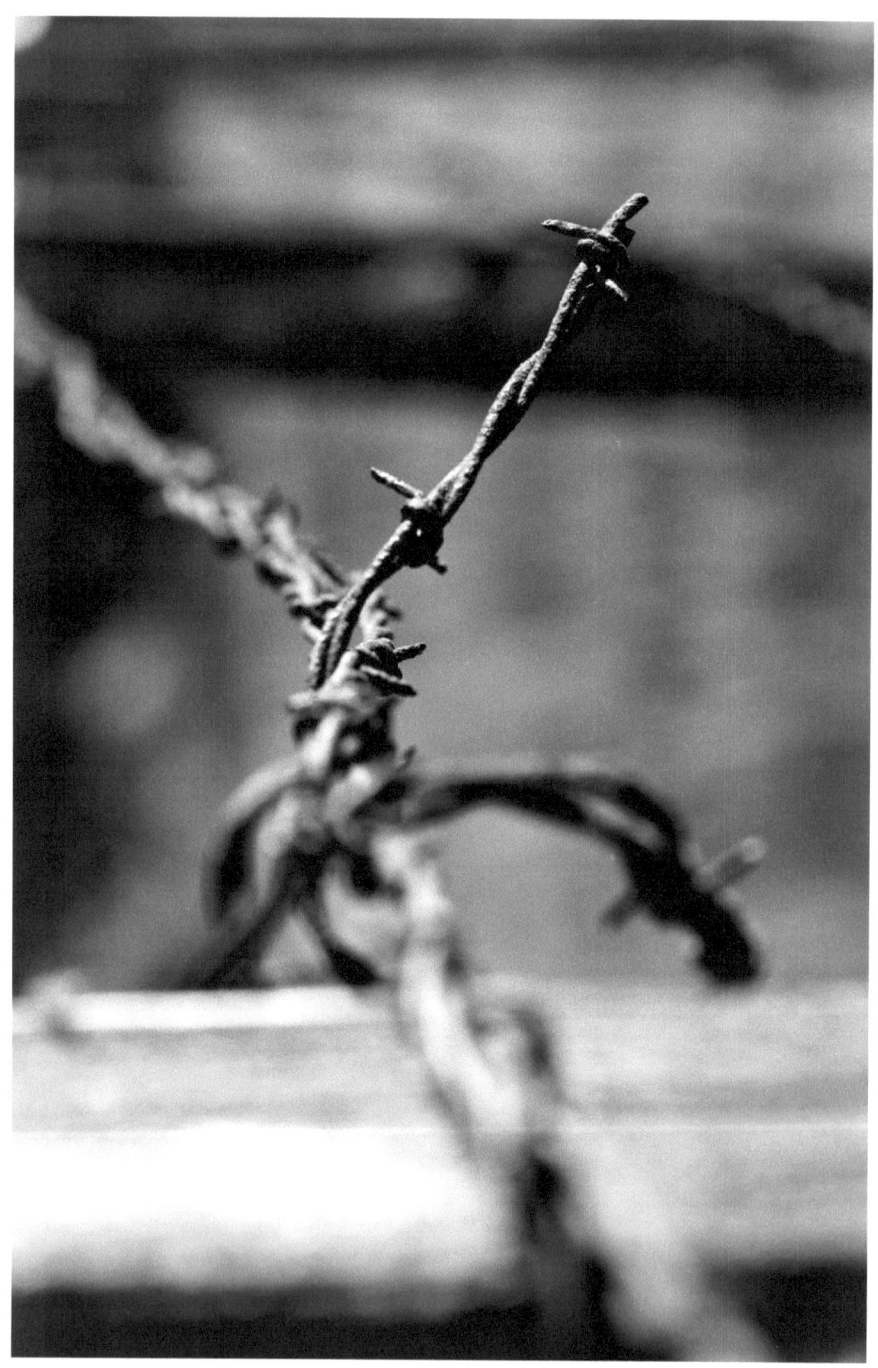

3359

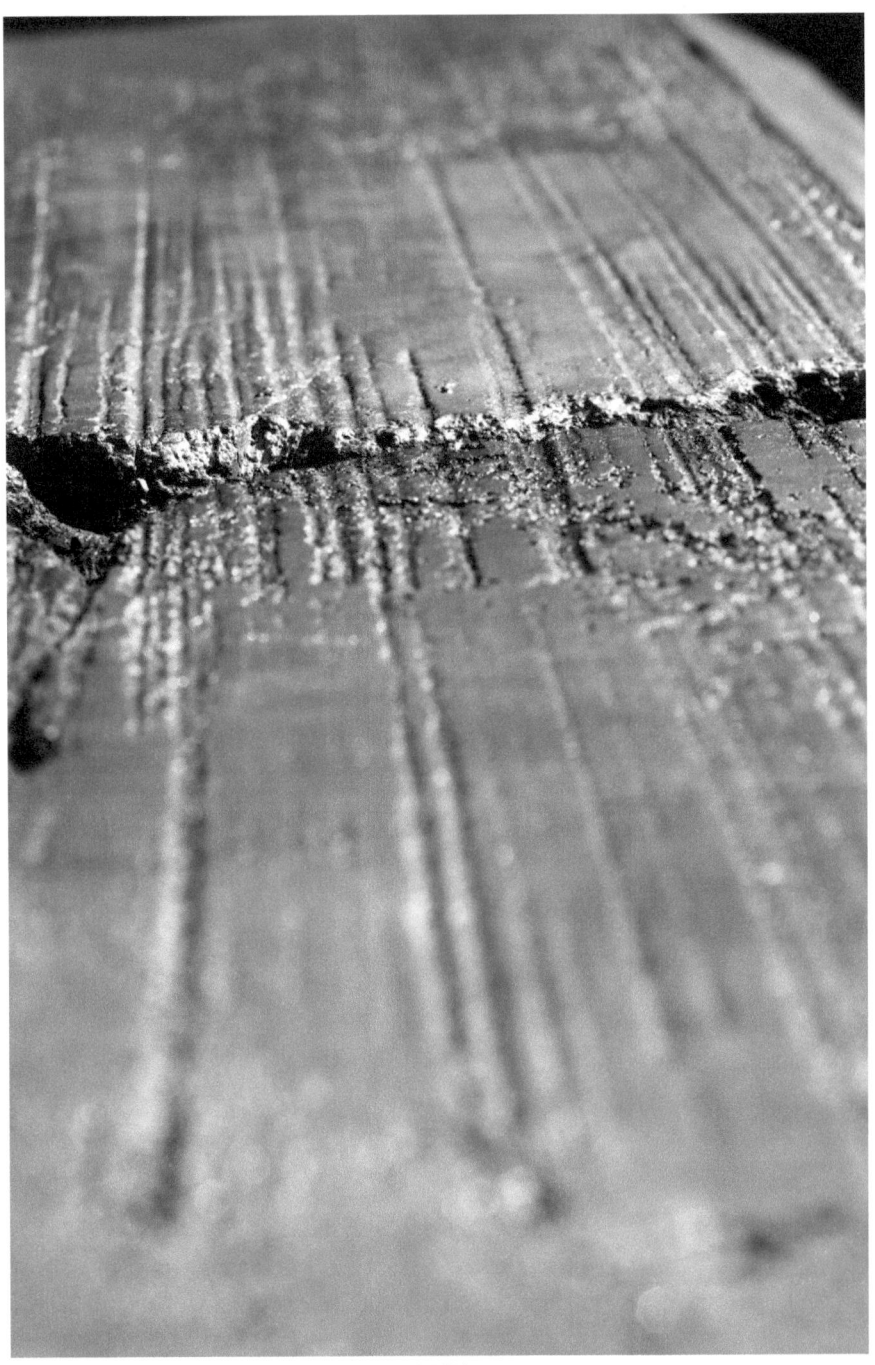

3656

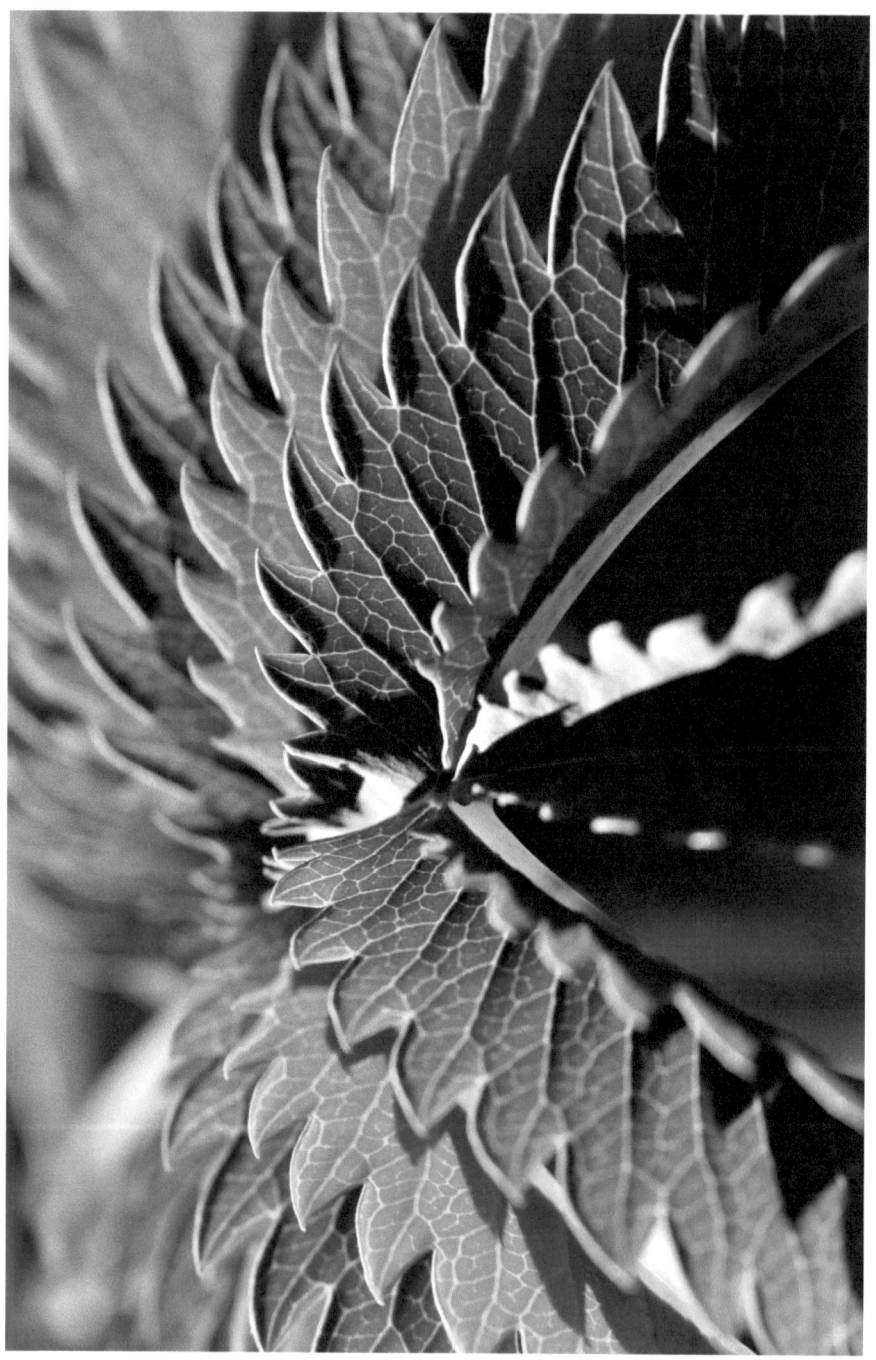

3714

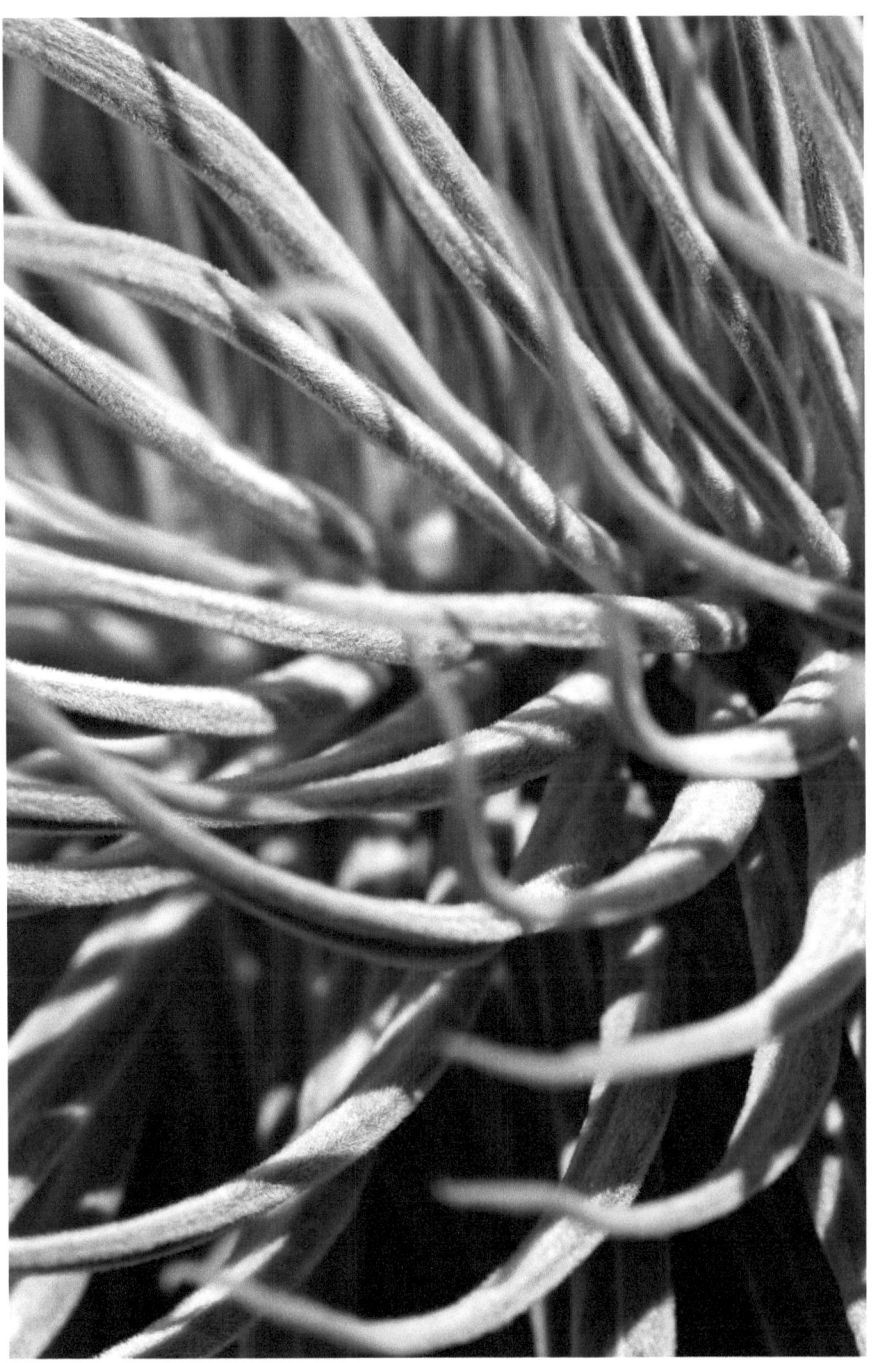

3752

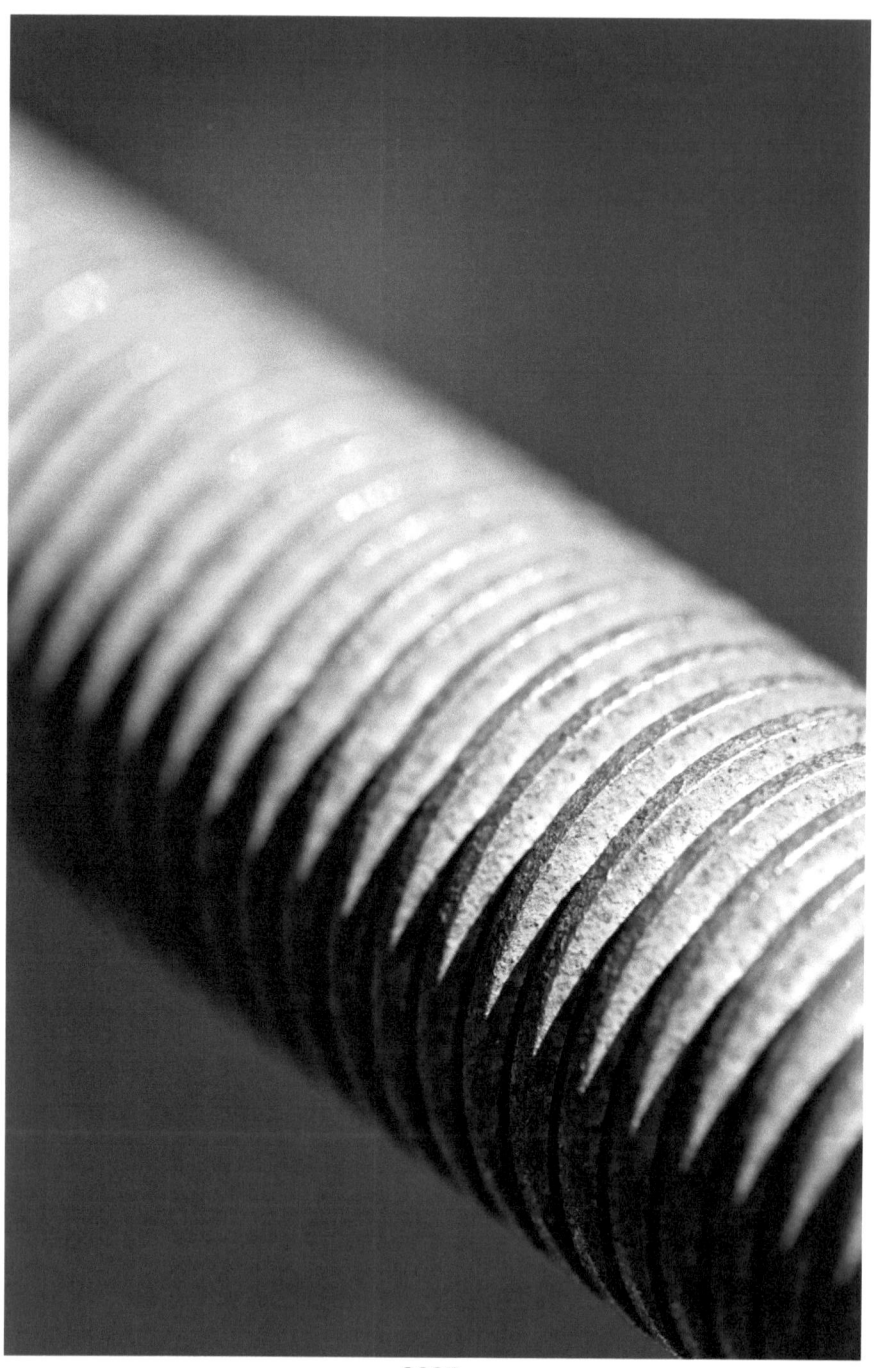

3937

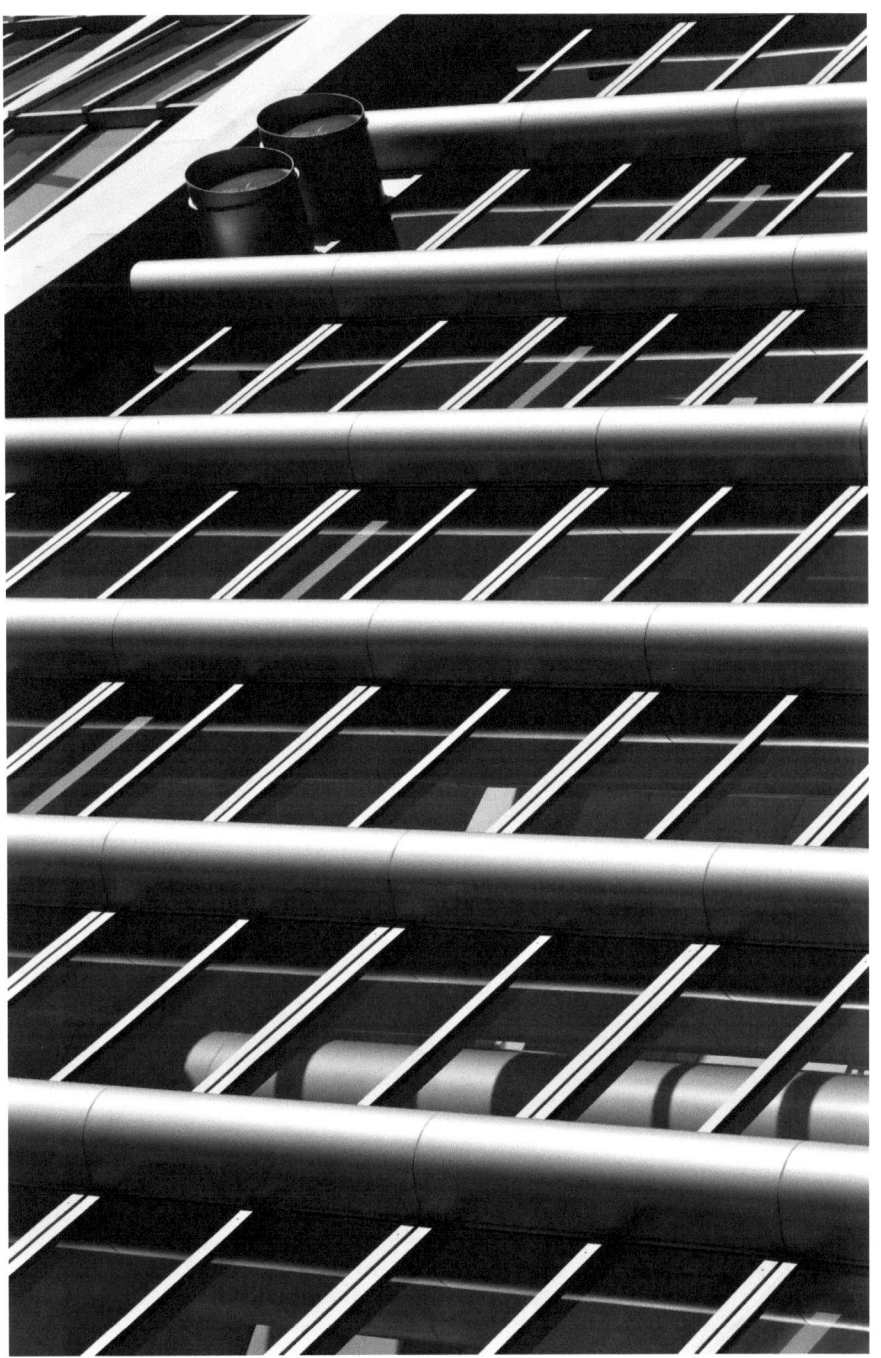

3943

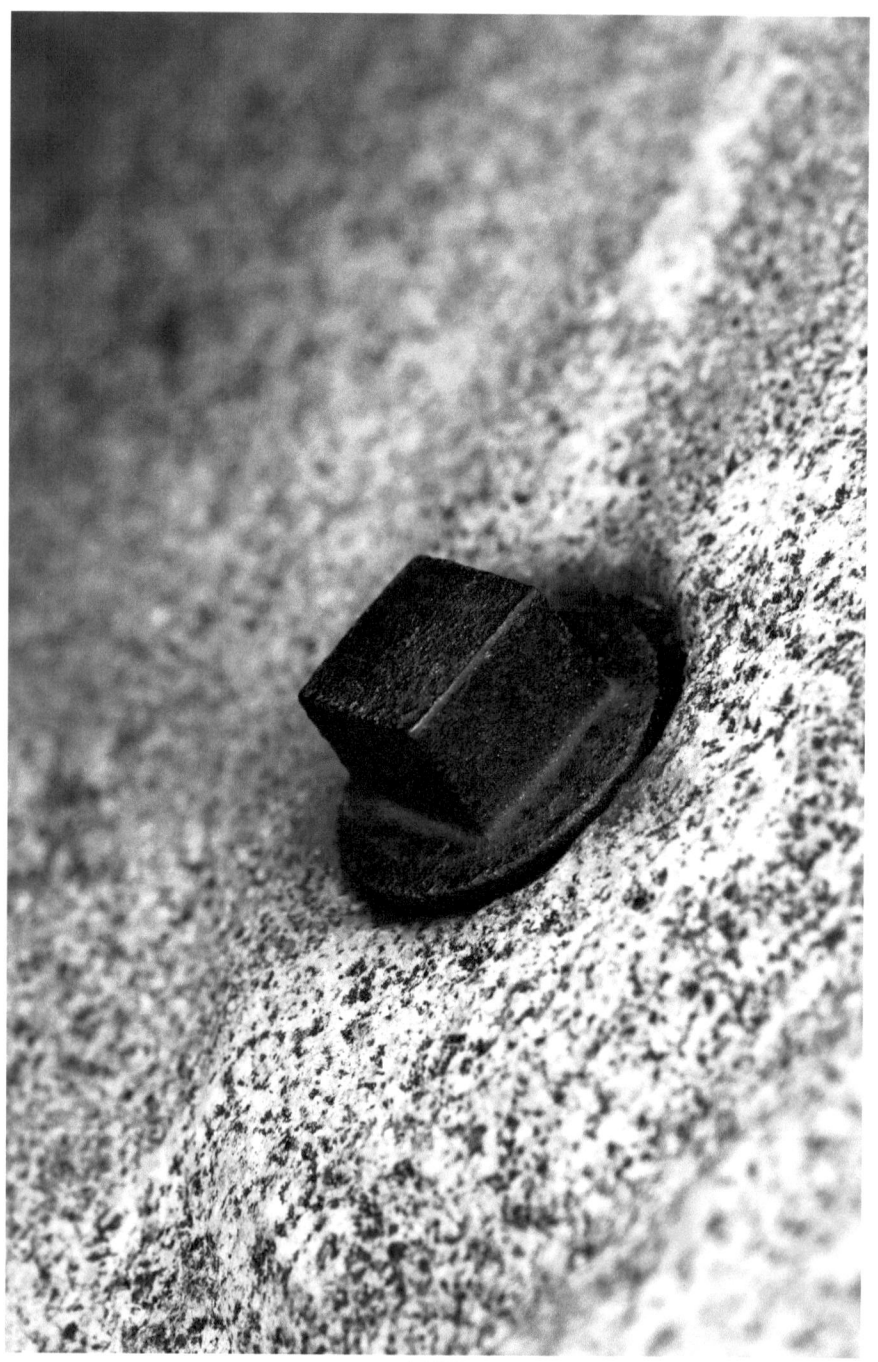

4035

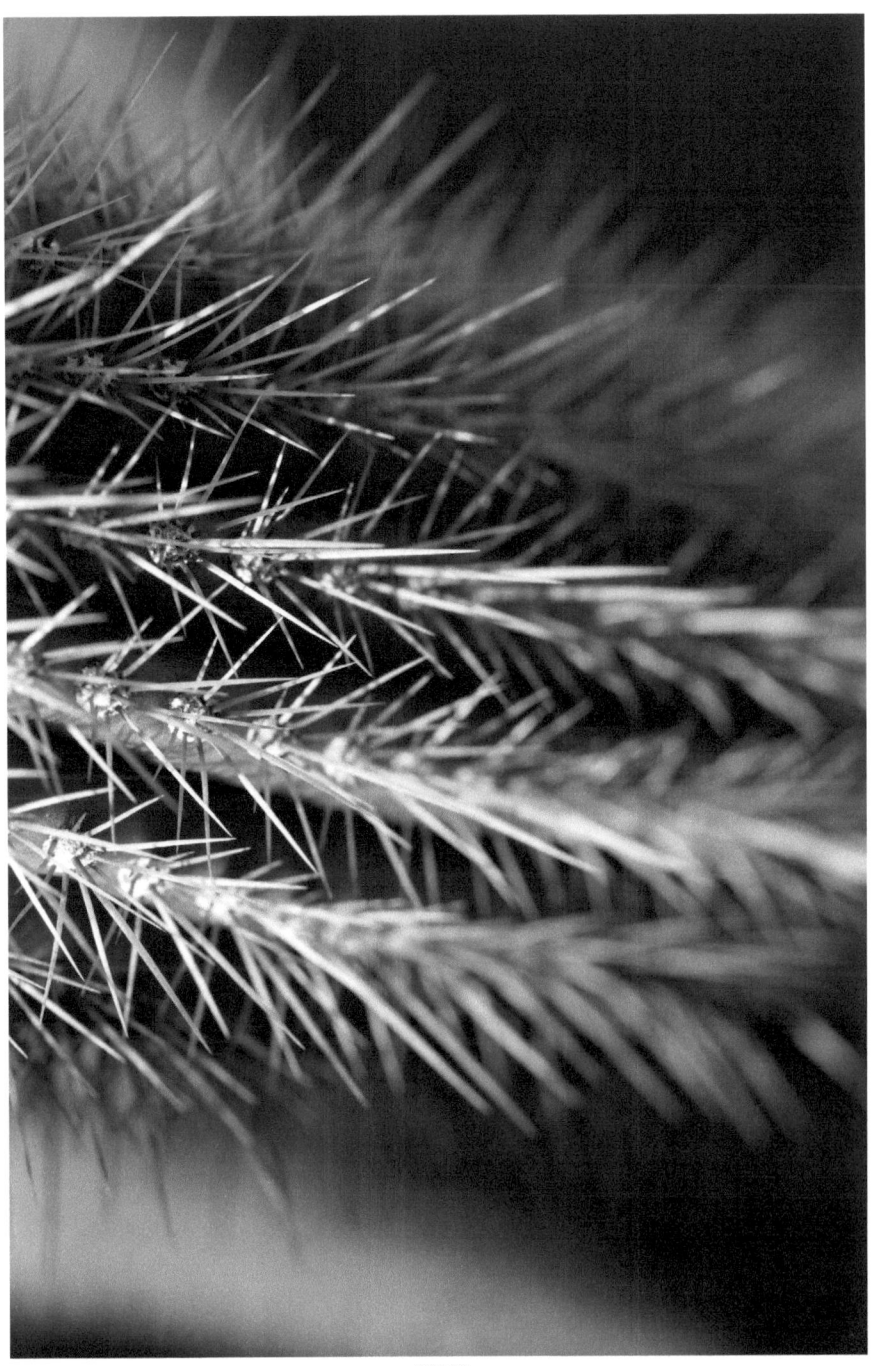

4070

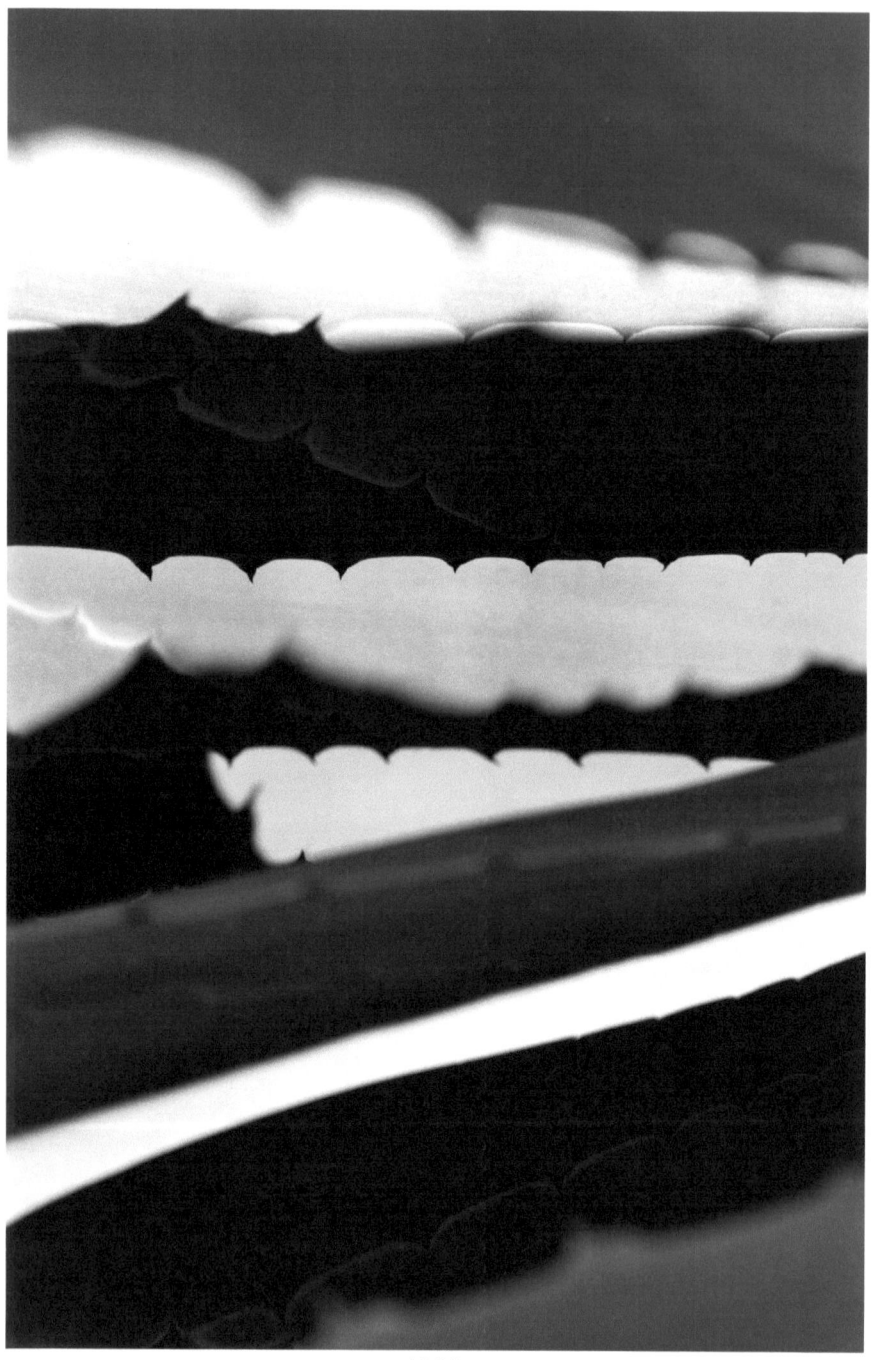

4099

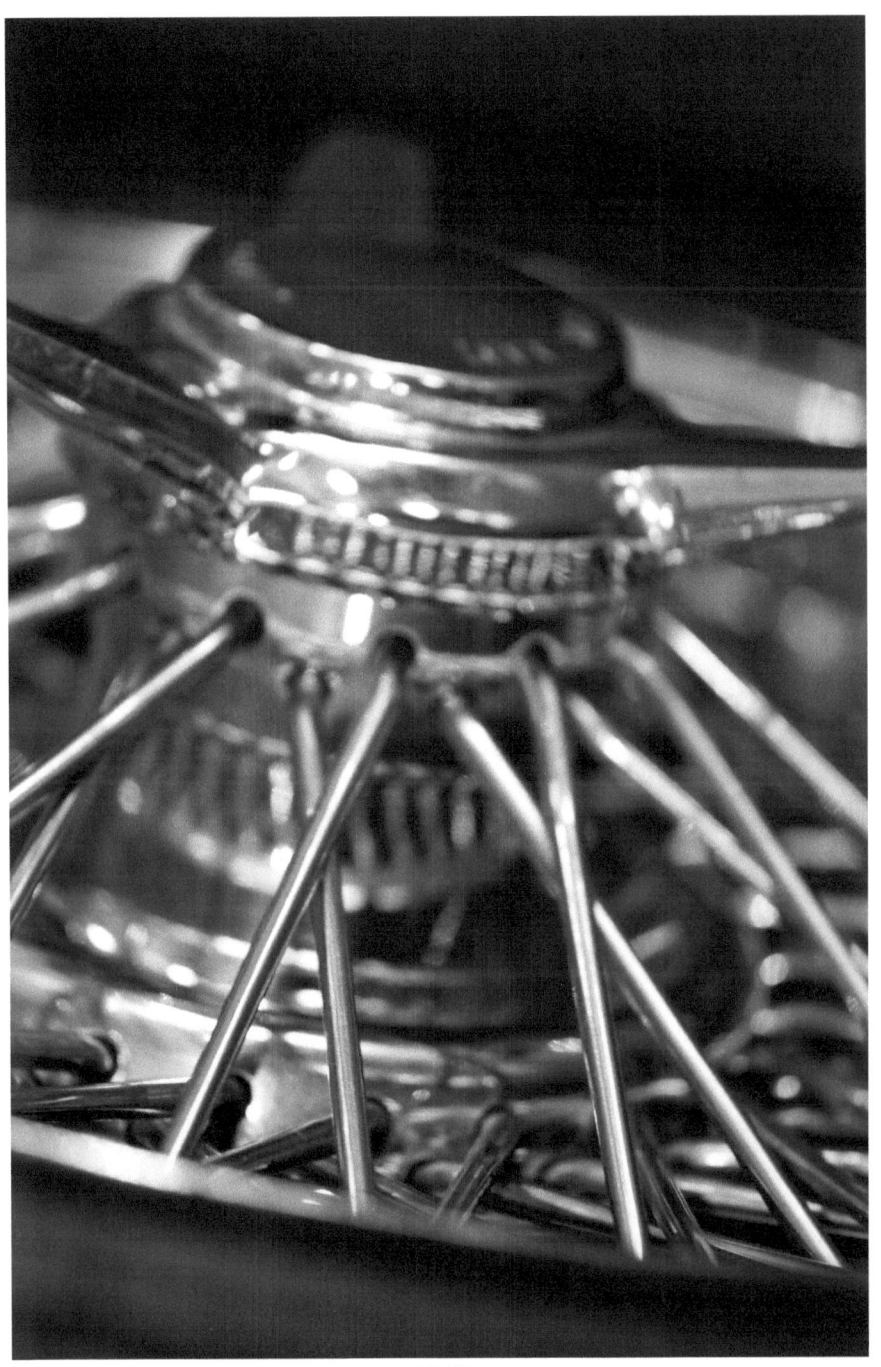

4193

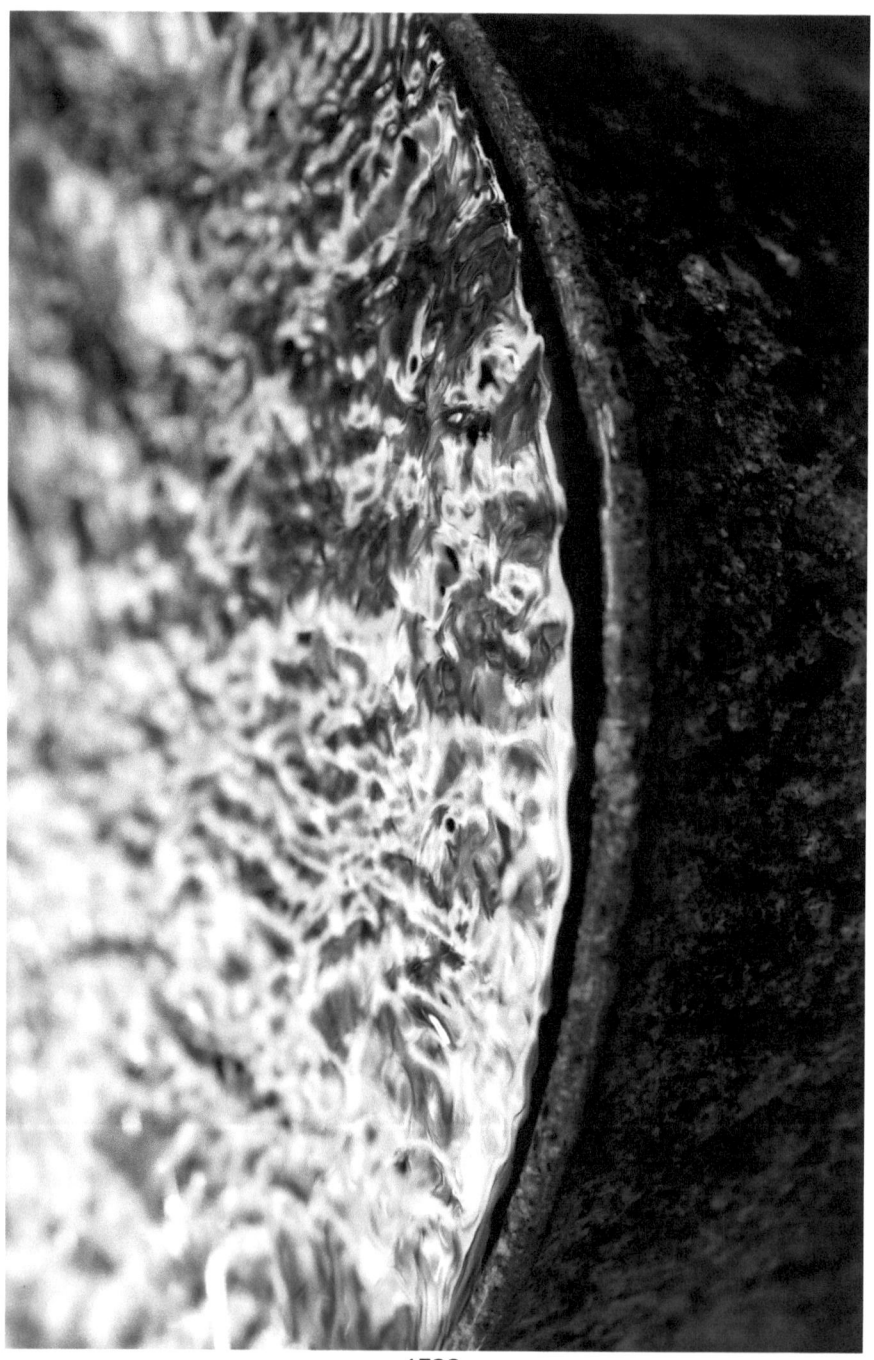

4533

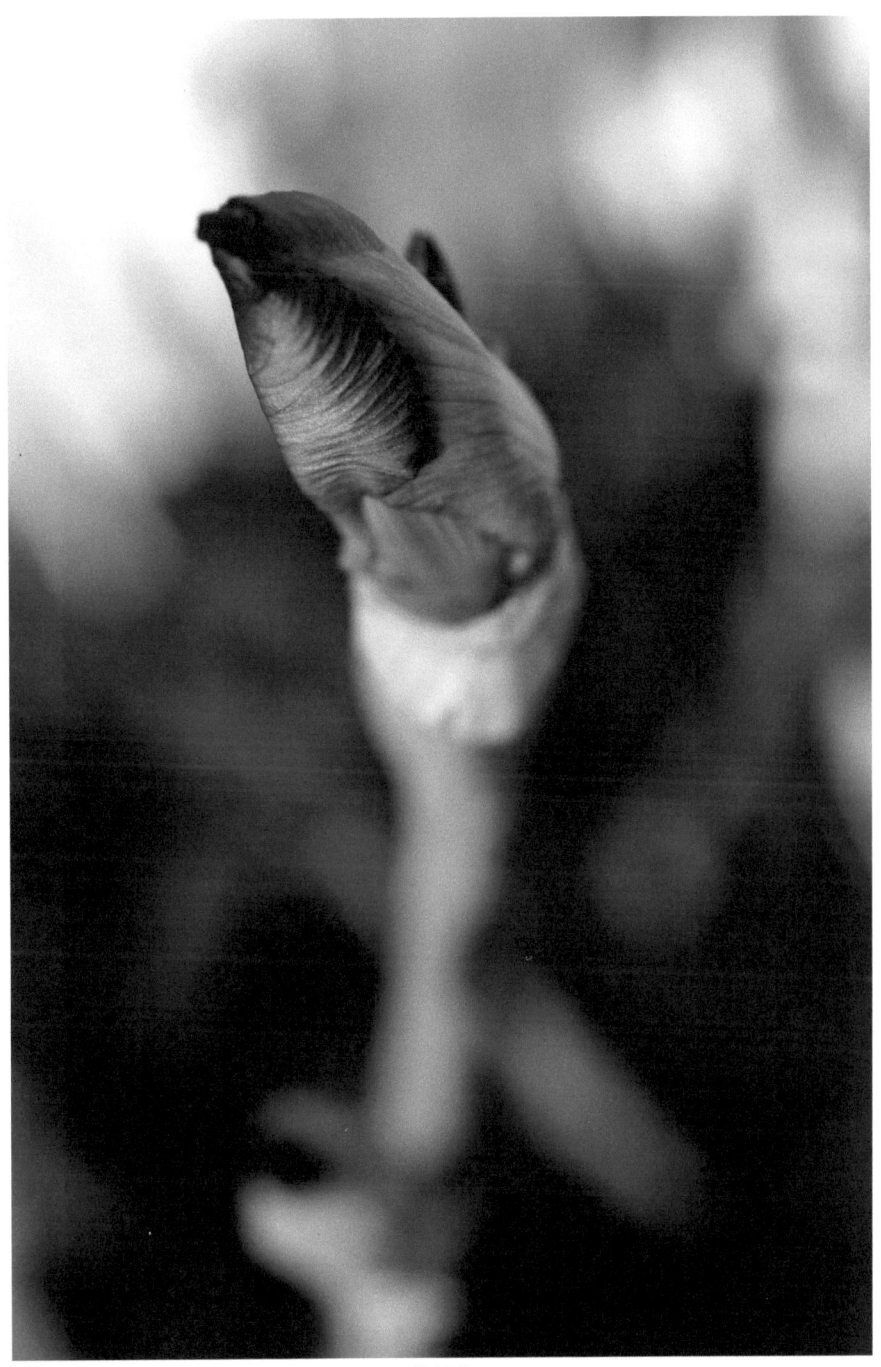

5492

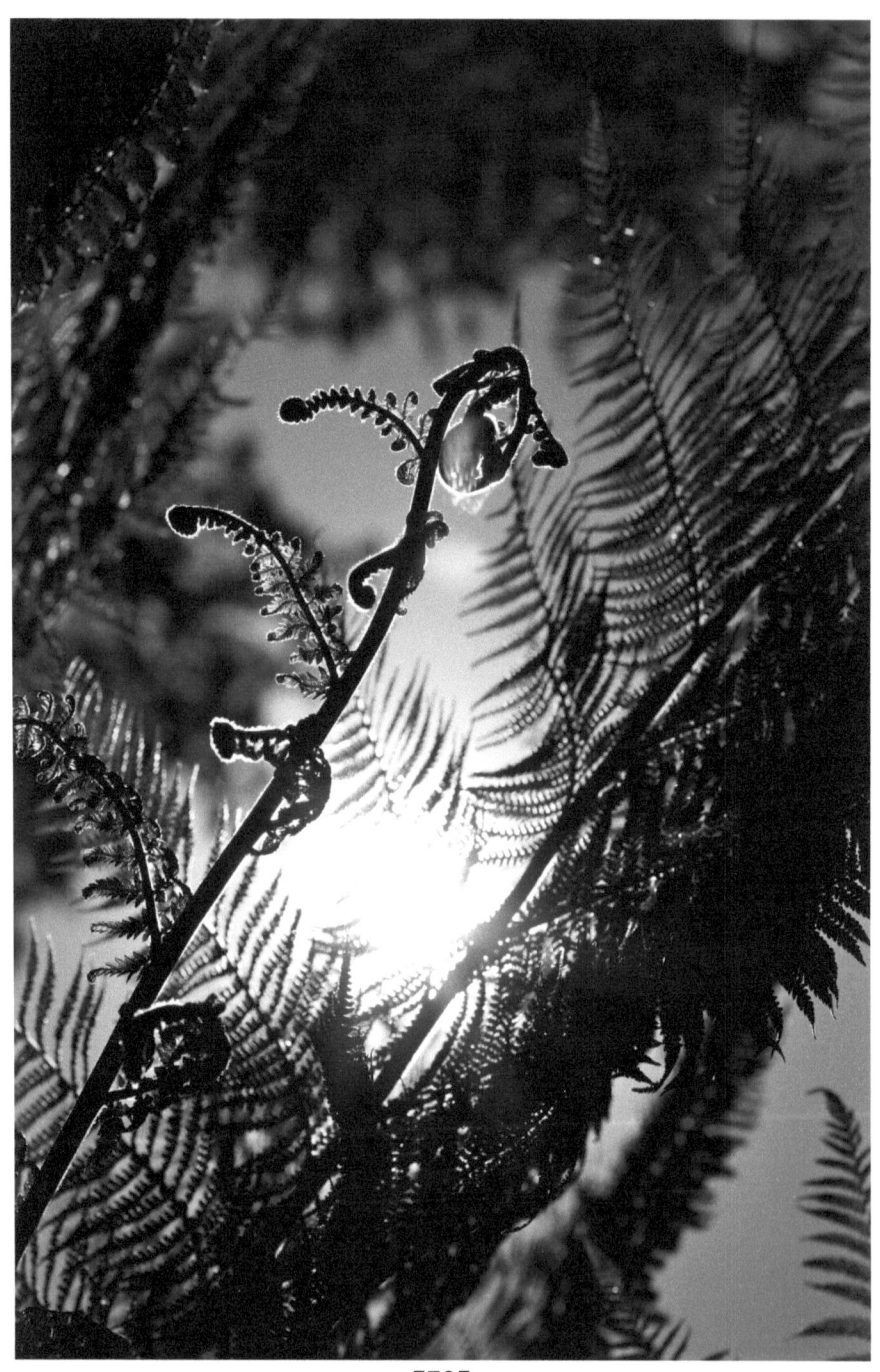

5705

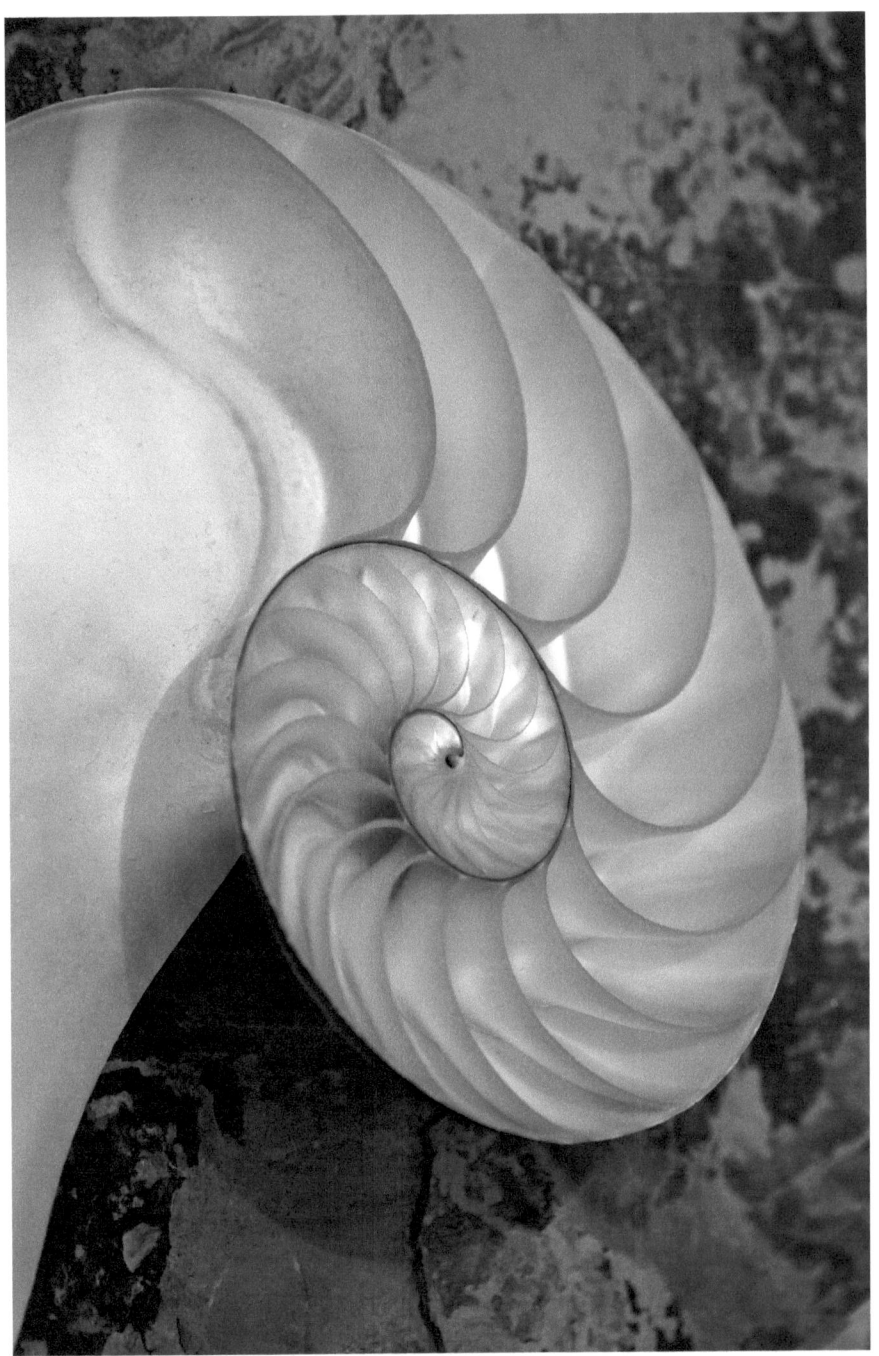

5708

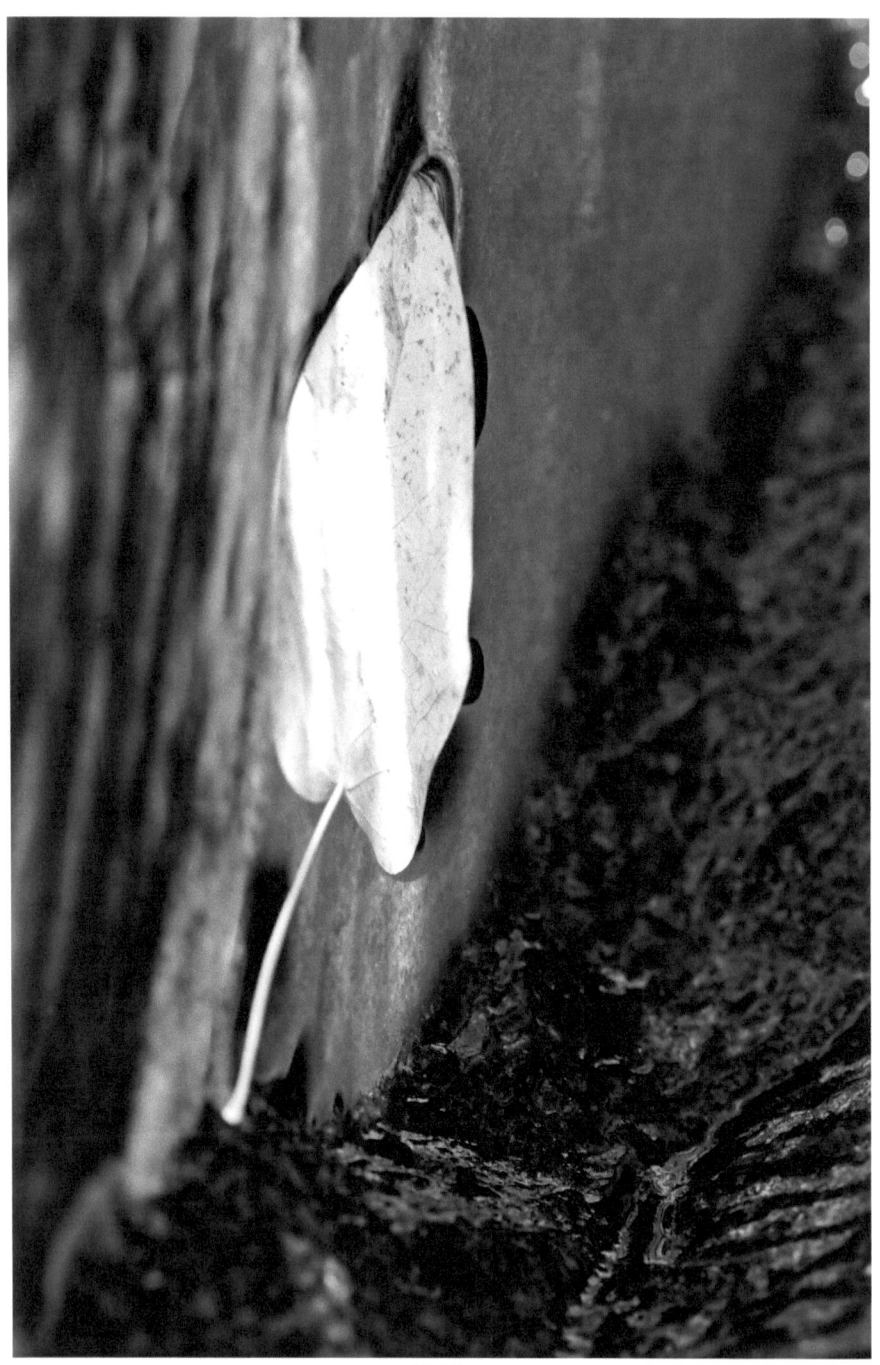

5750

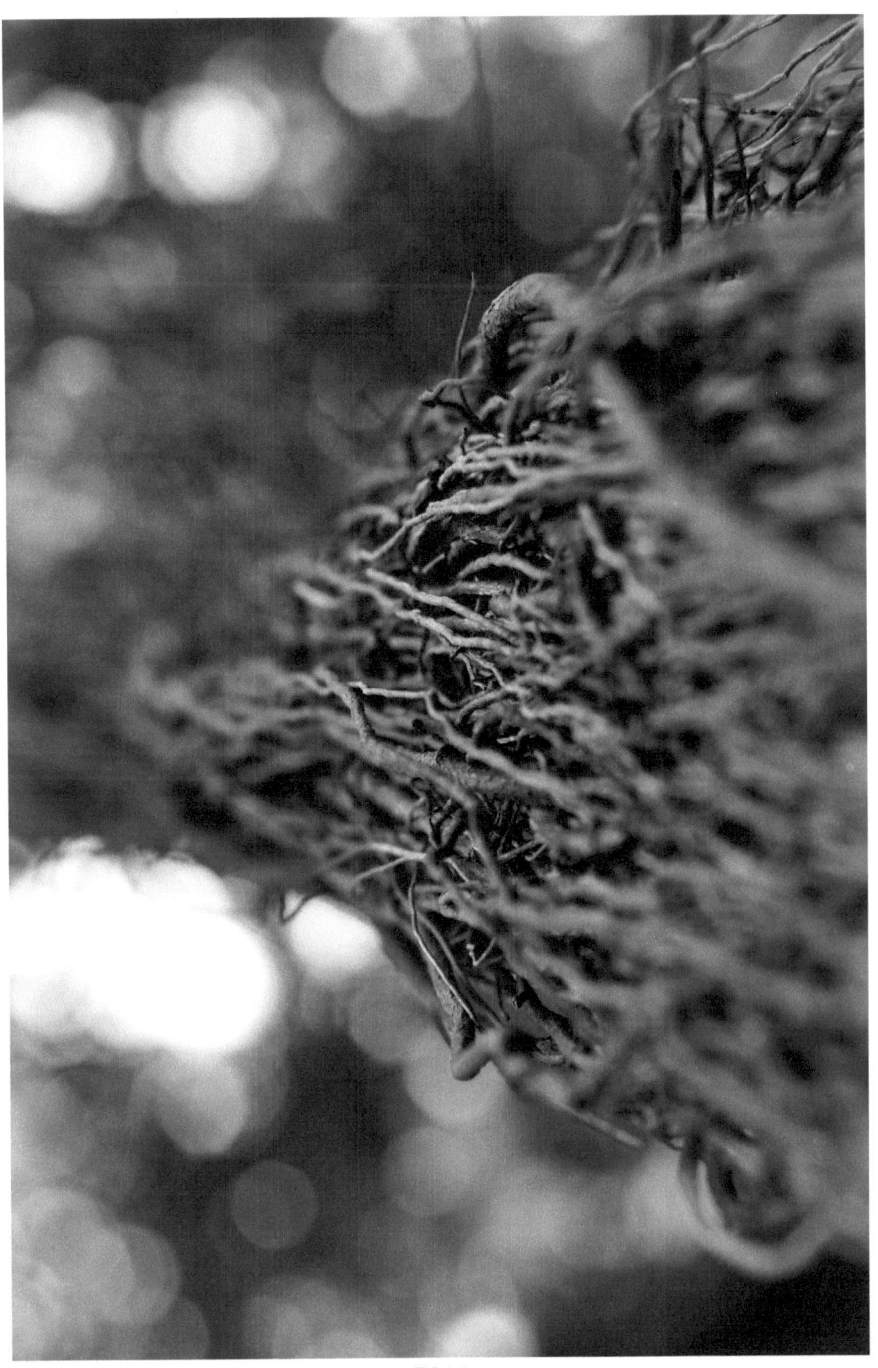

5811

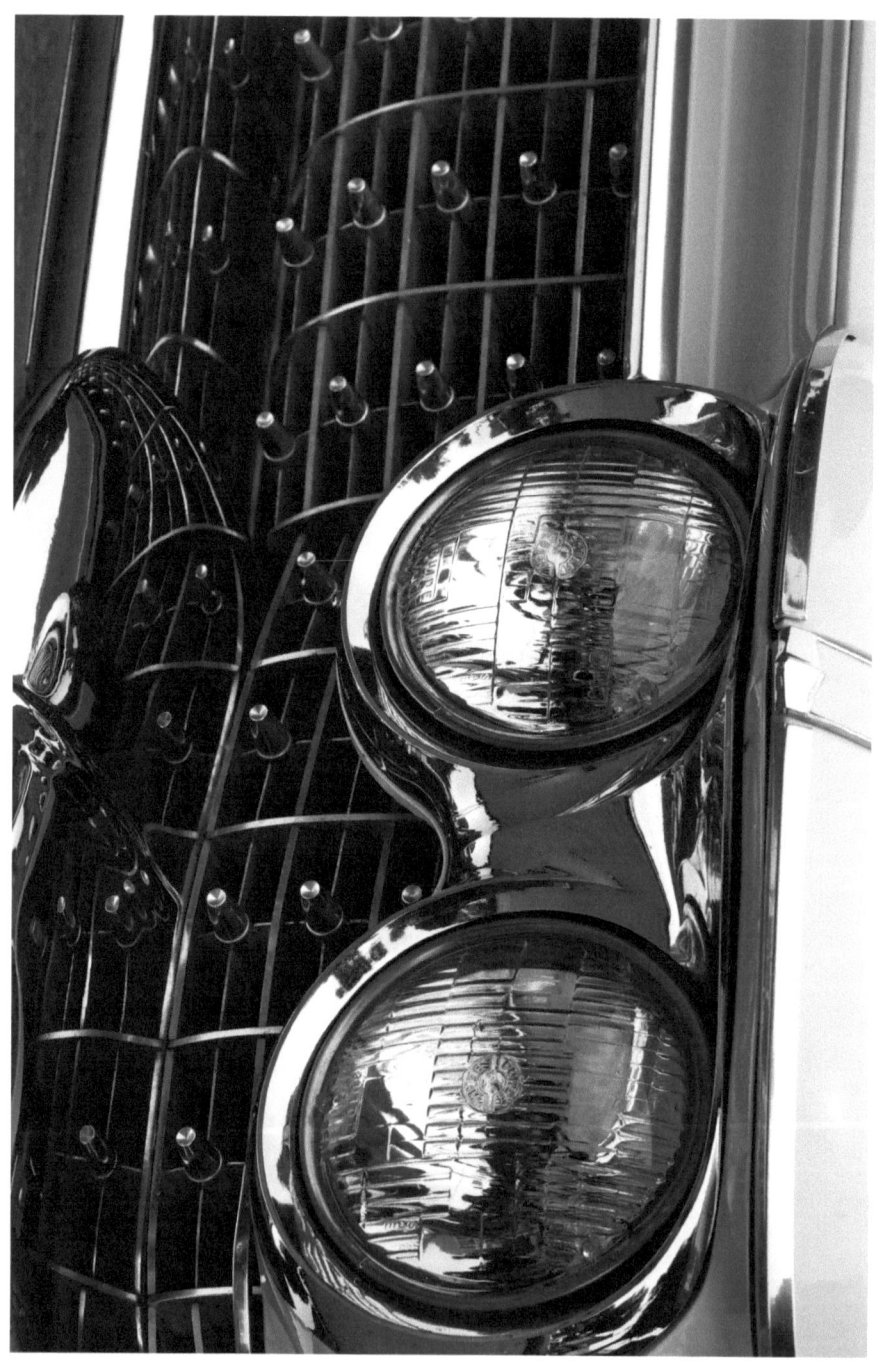

5844

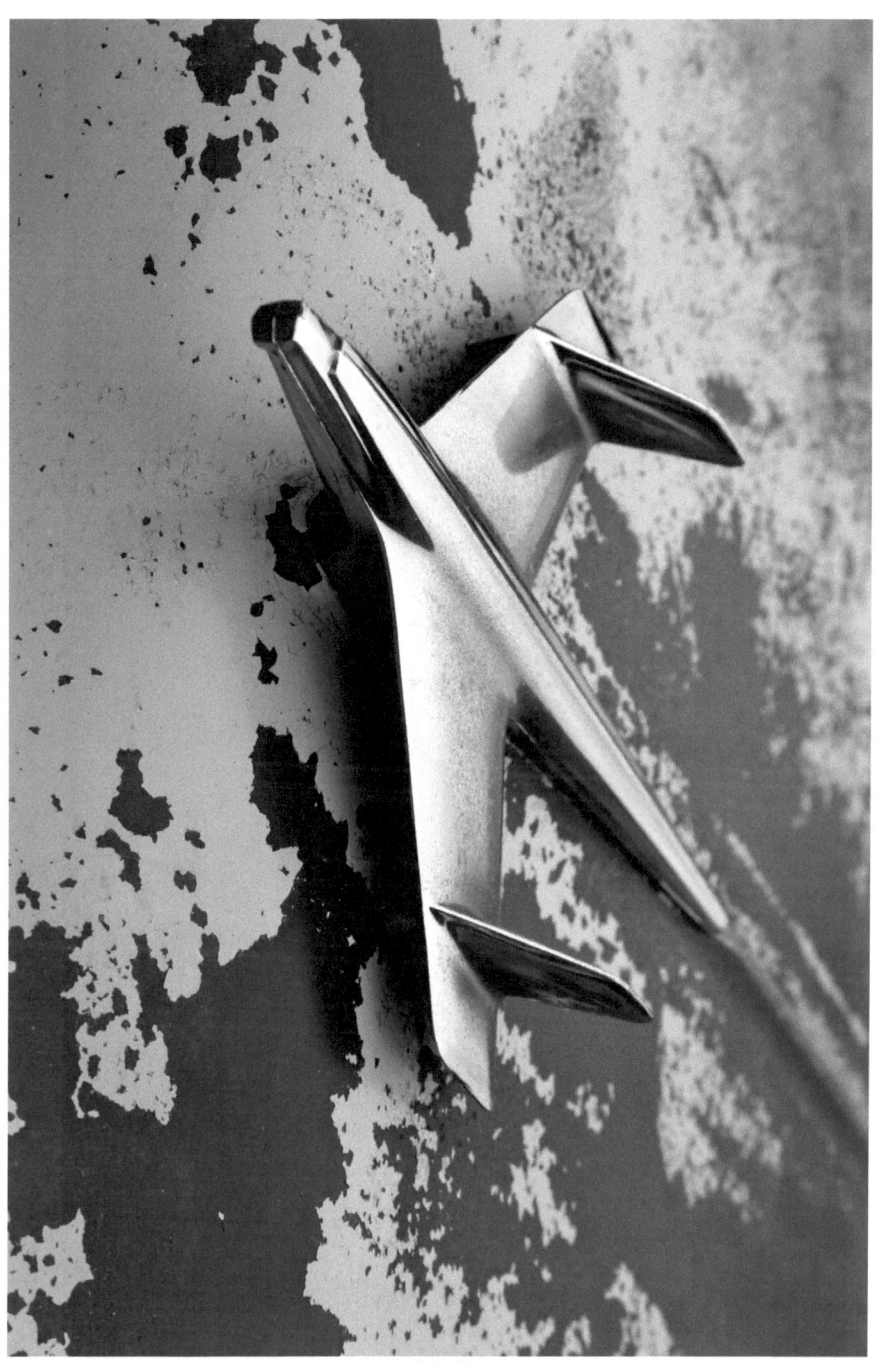

5846

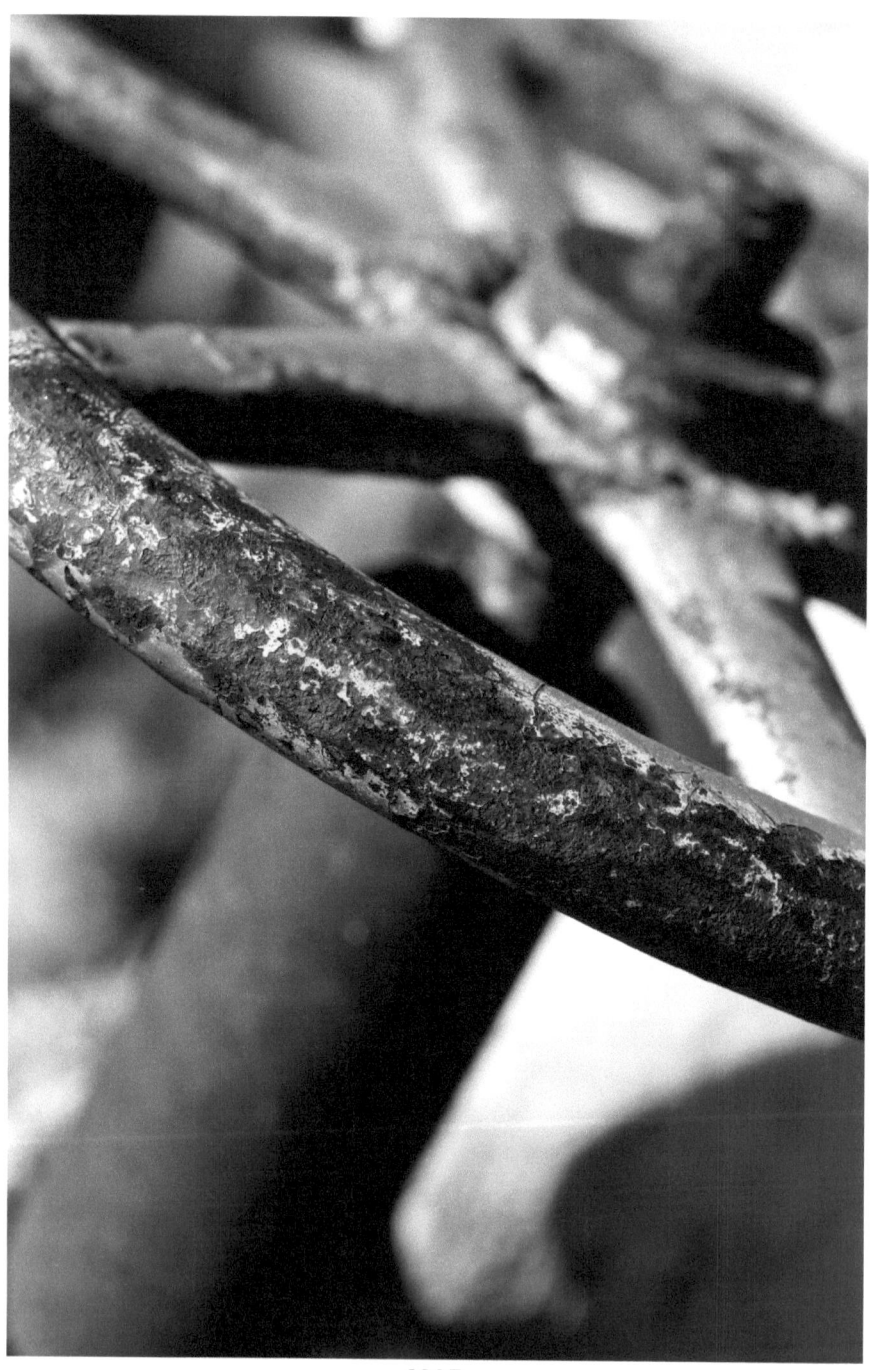

6095

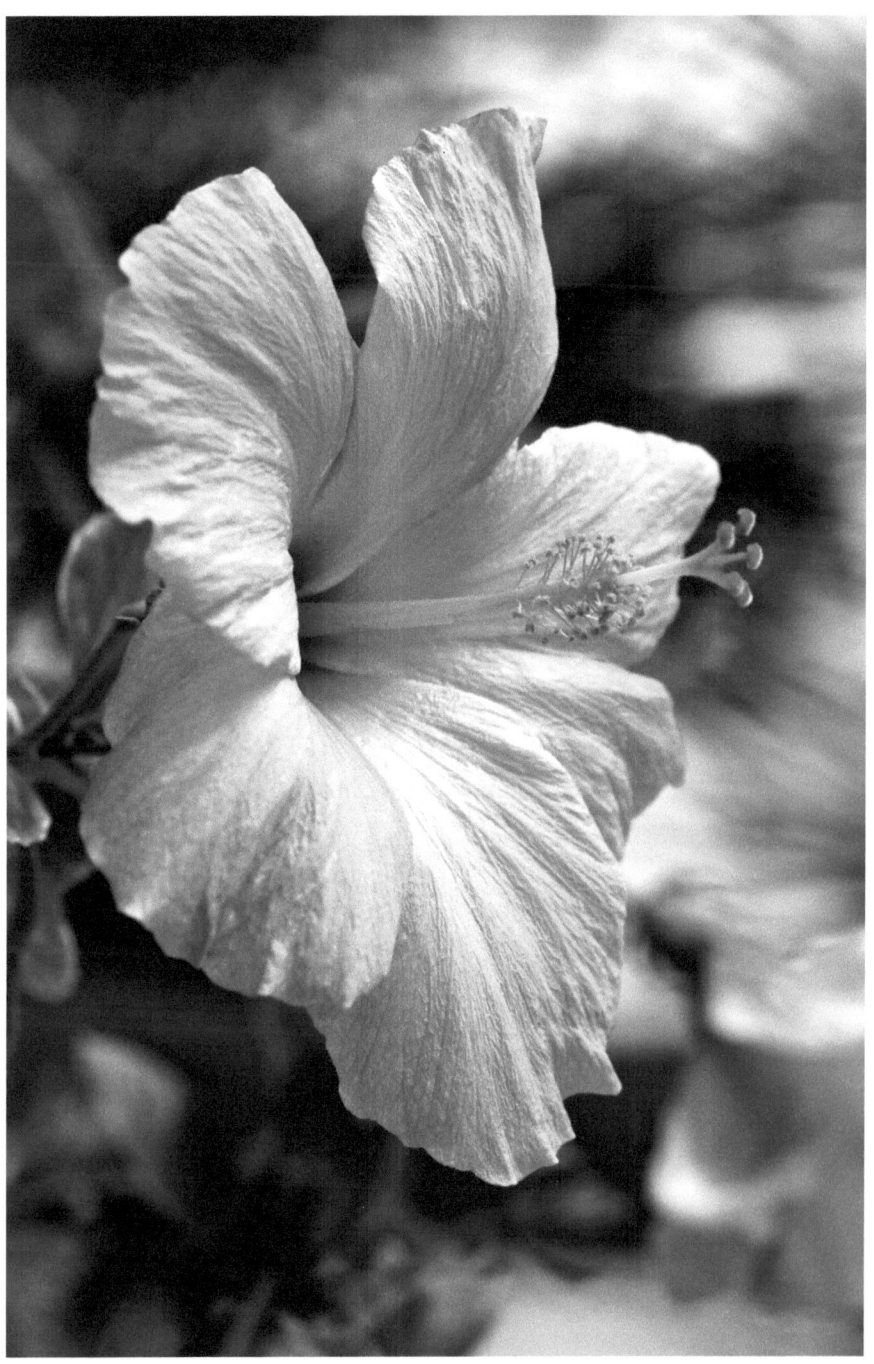

6990

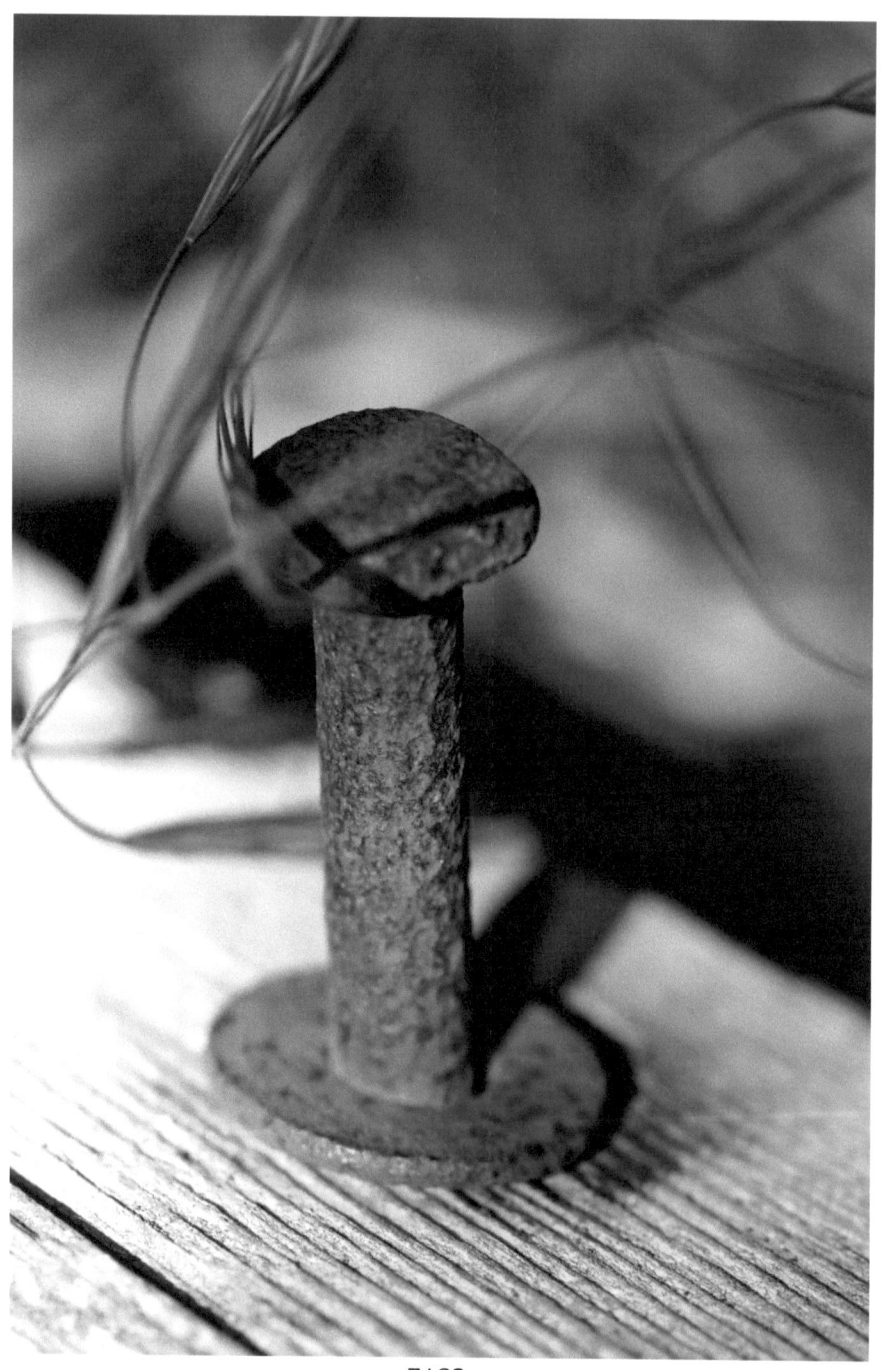

7182

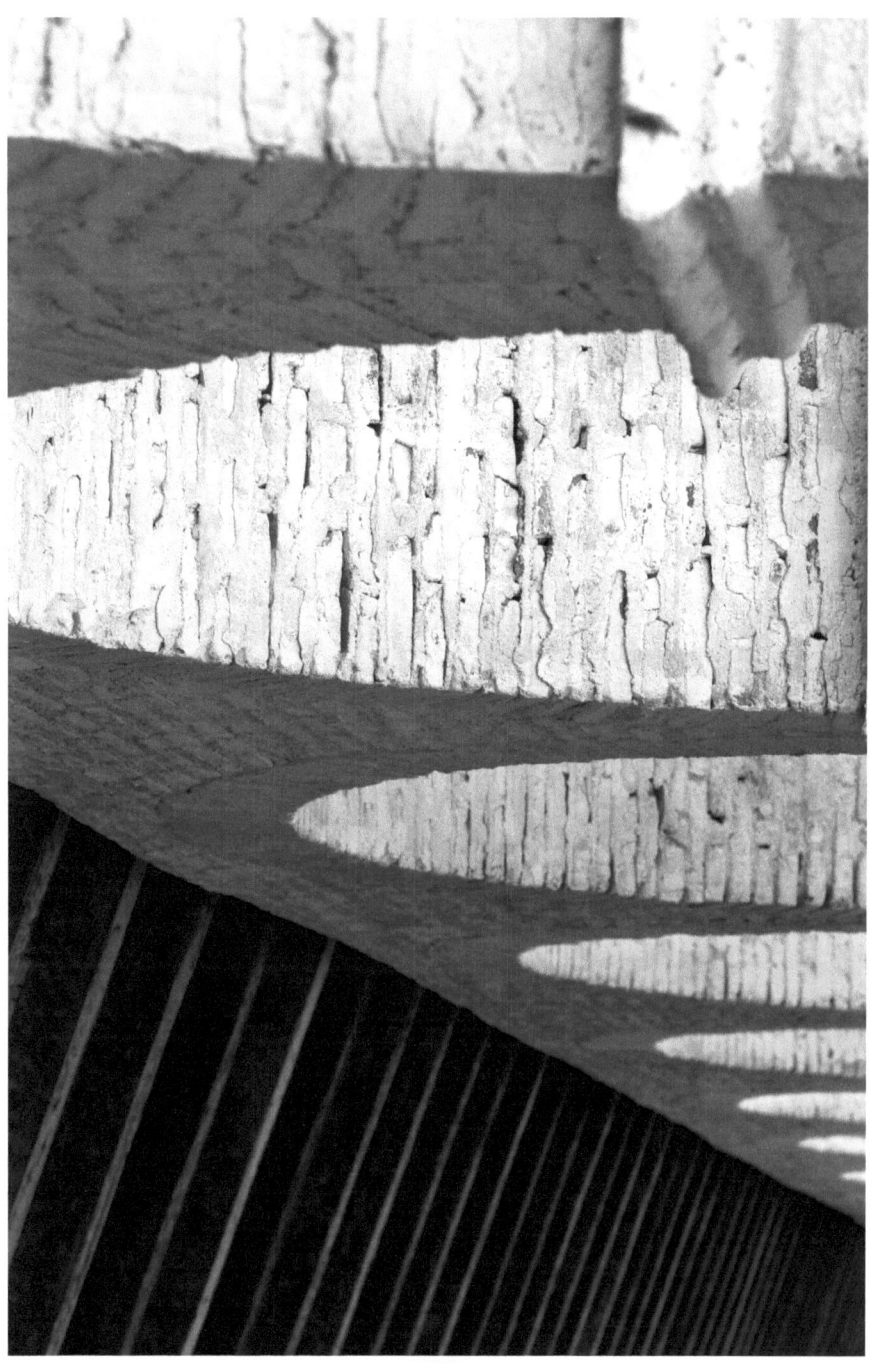

7656

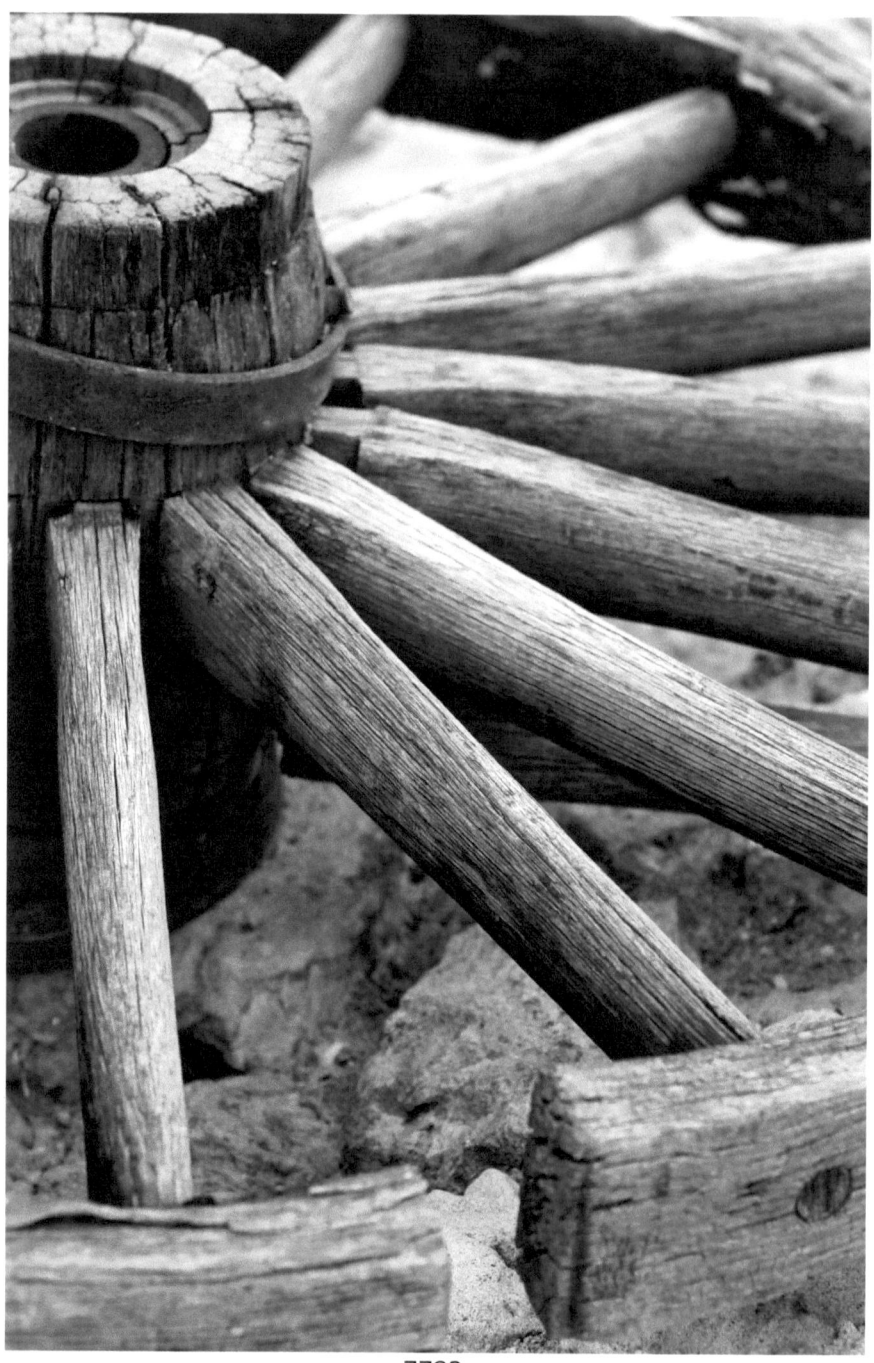

7783

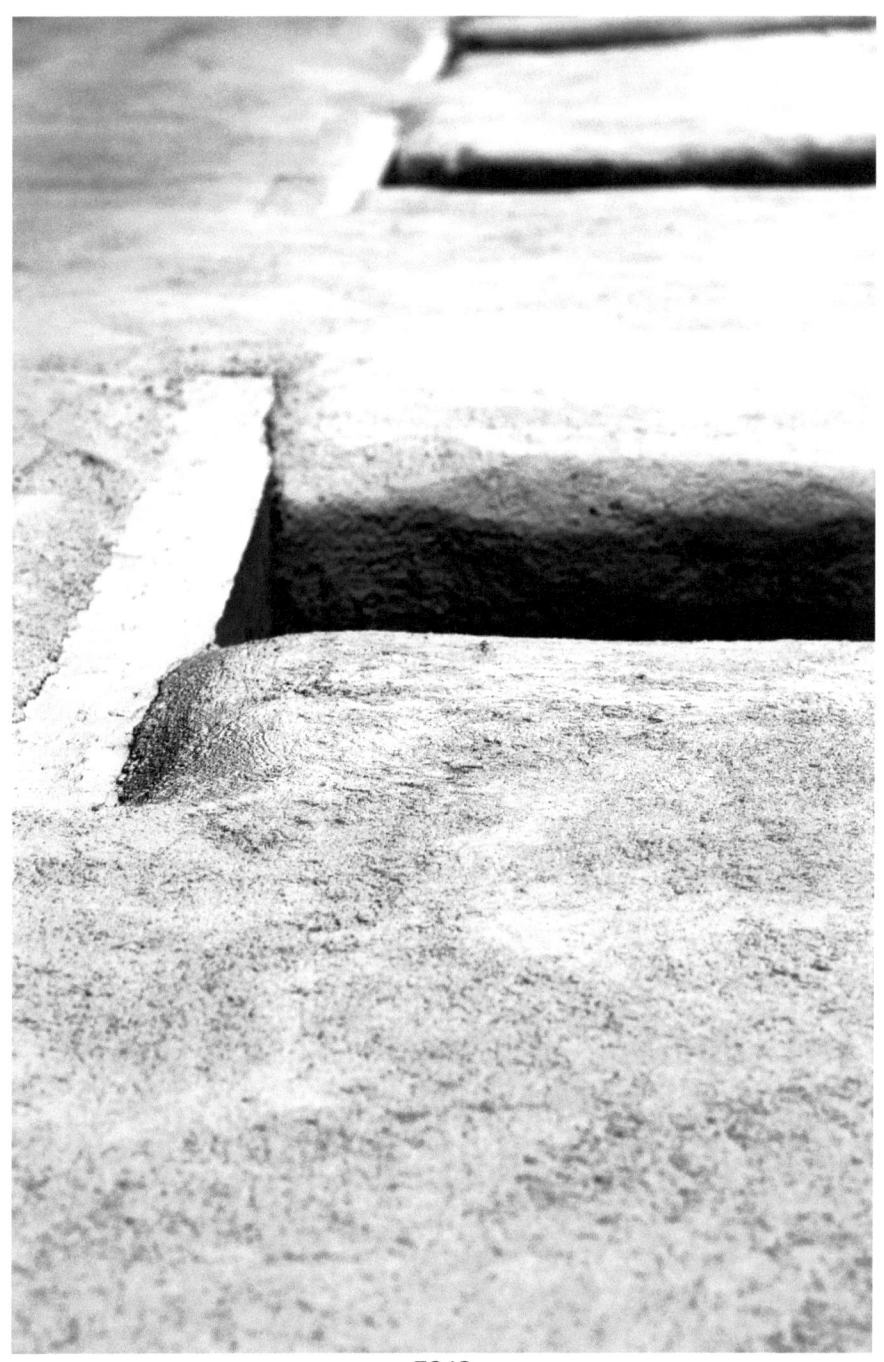

7843

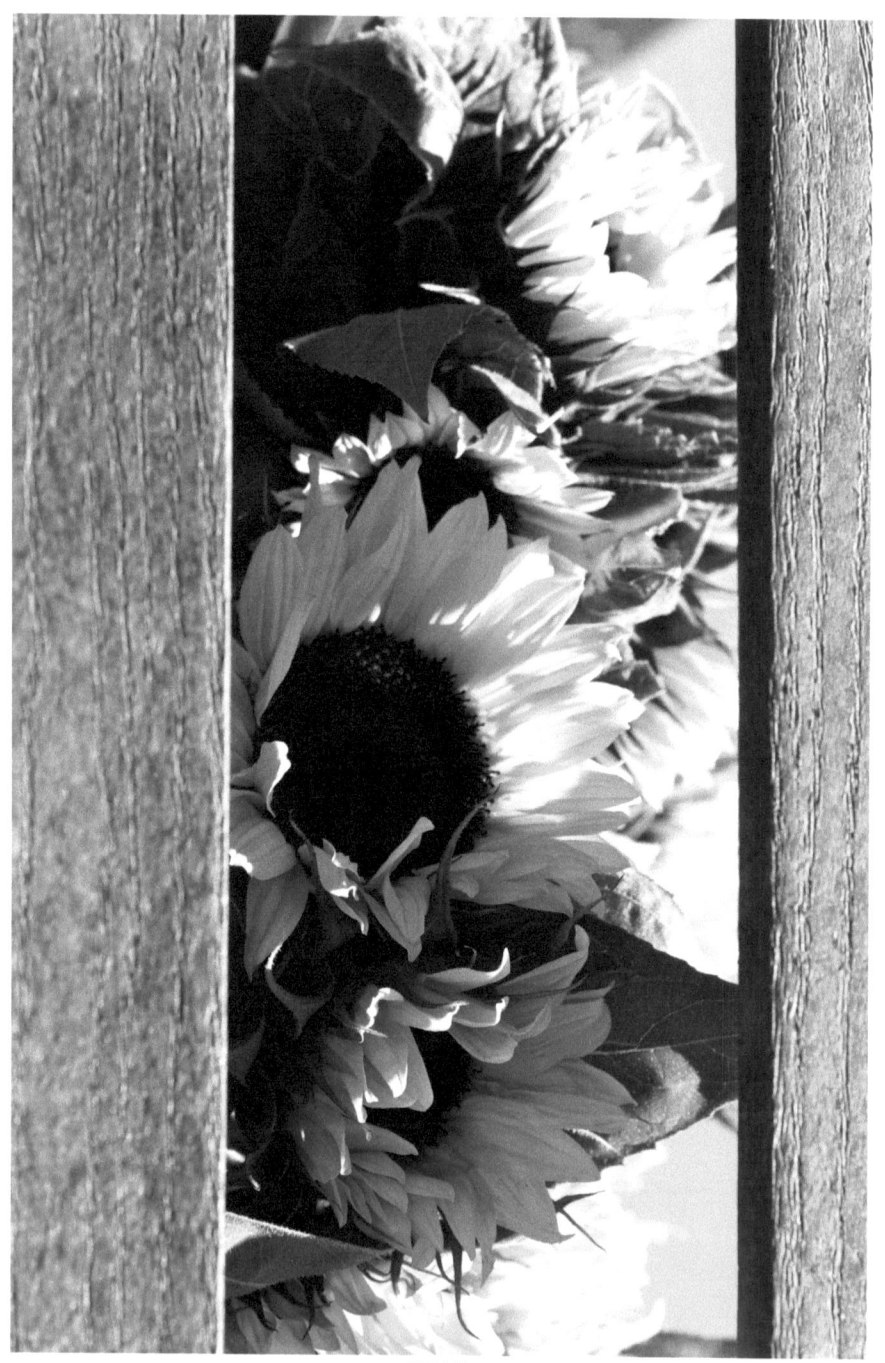

8345

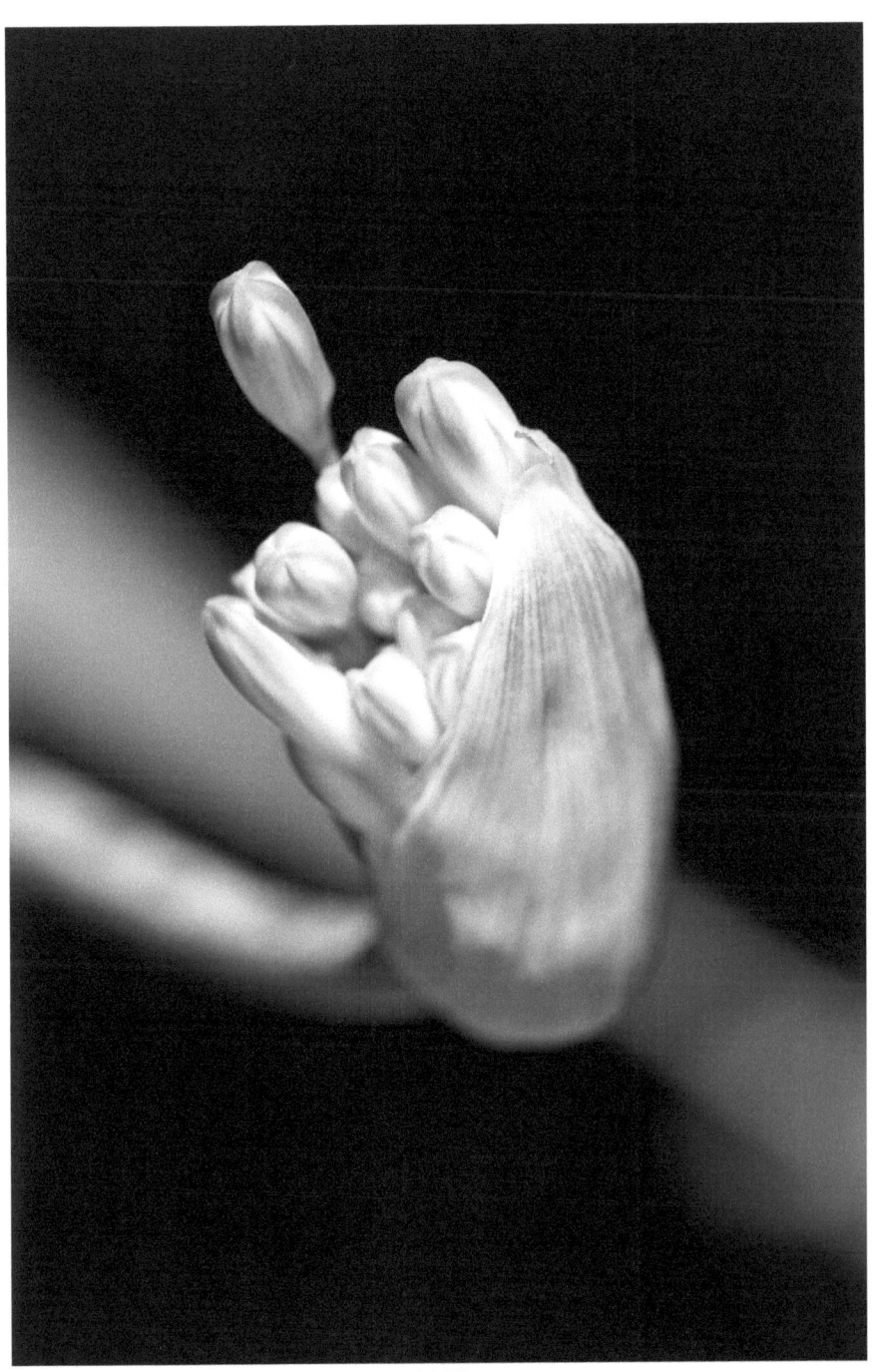

8407

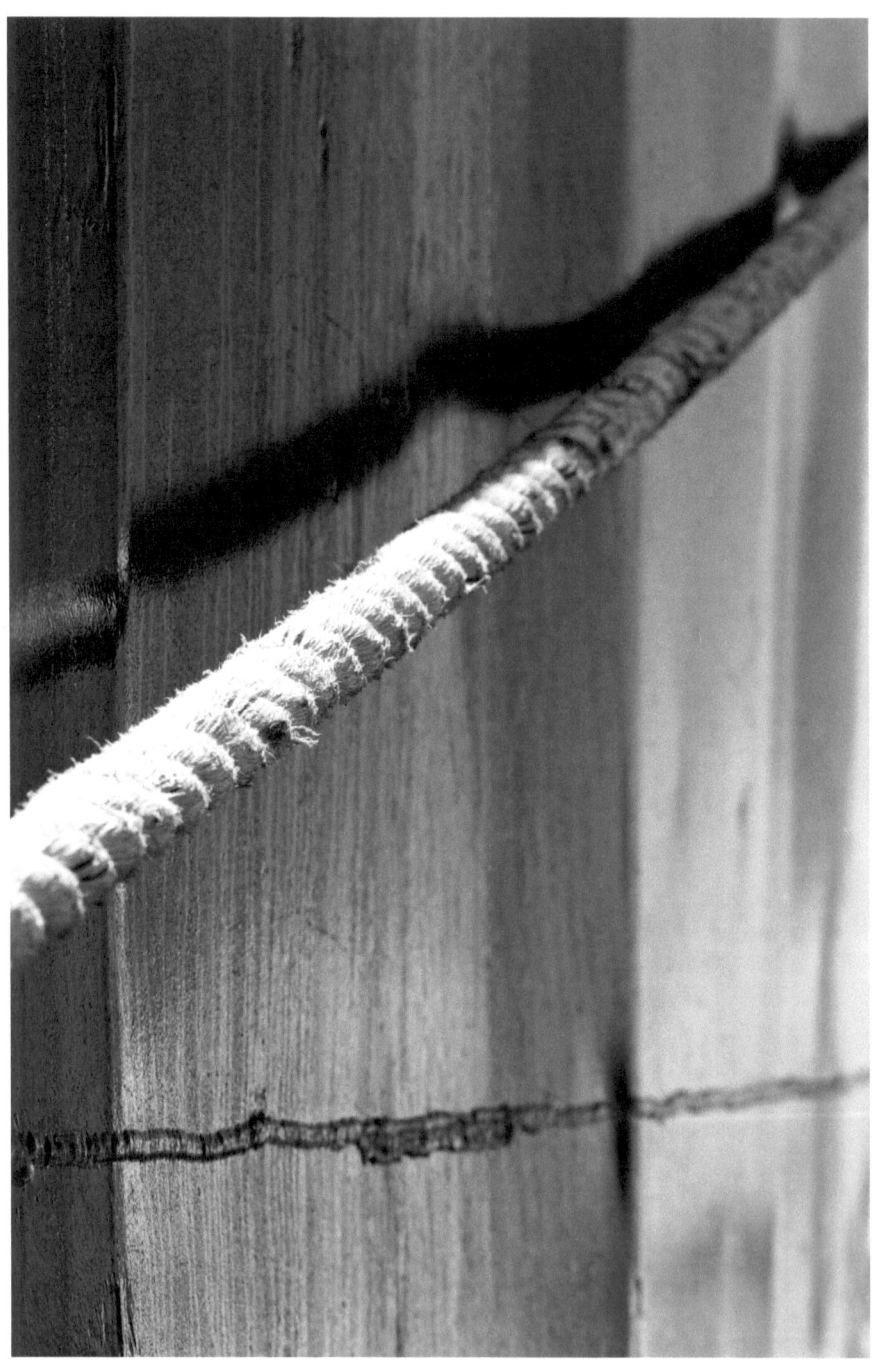

8470

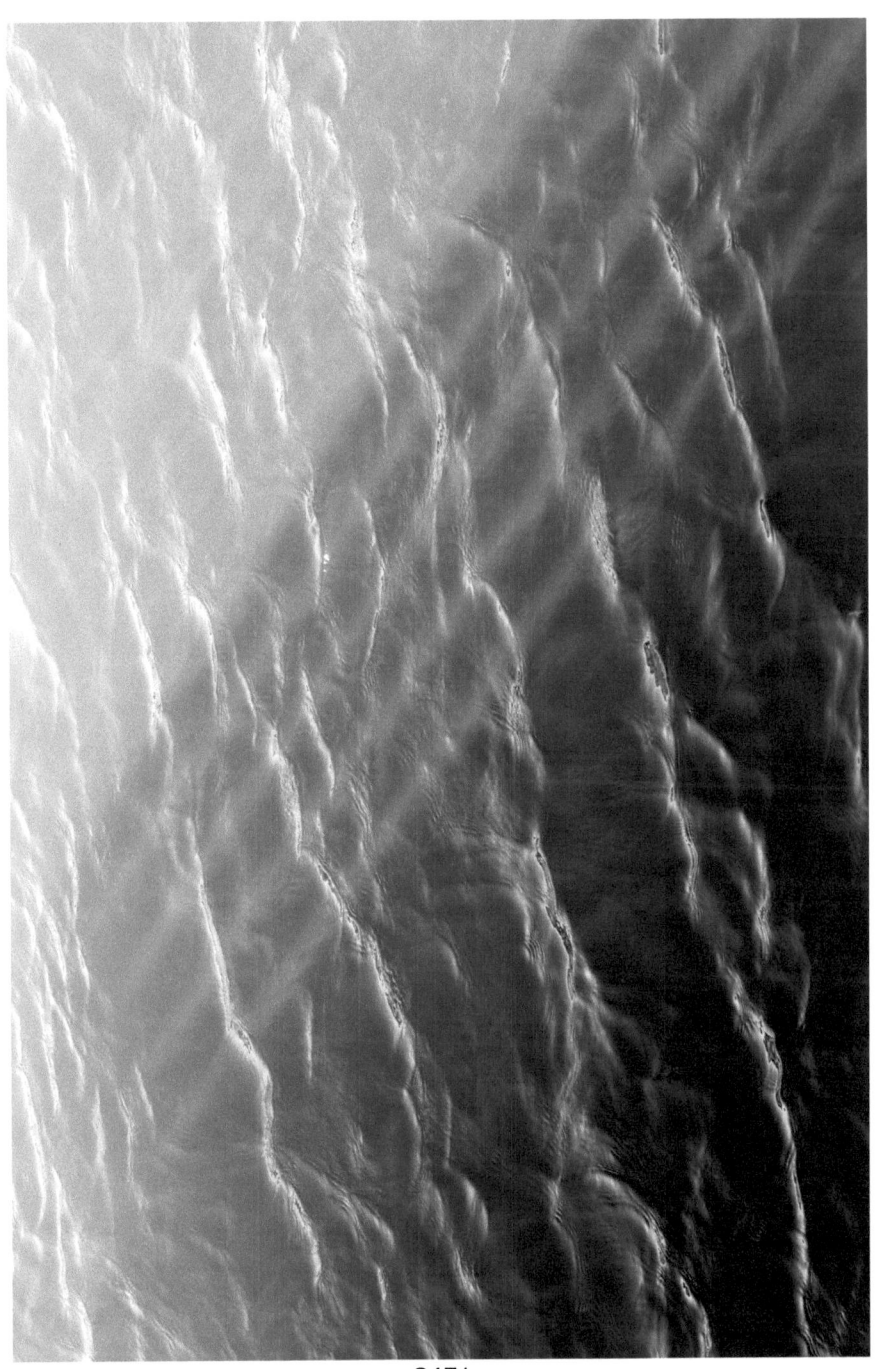

8471

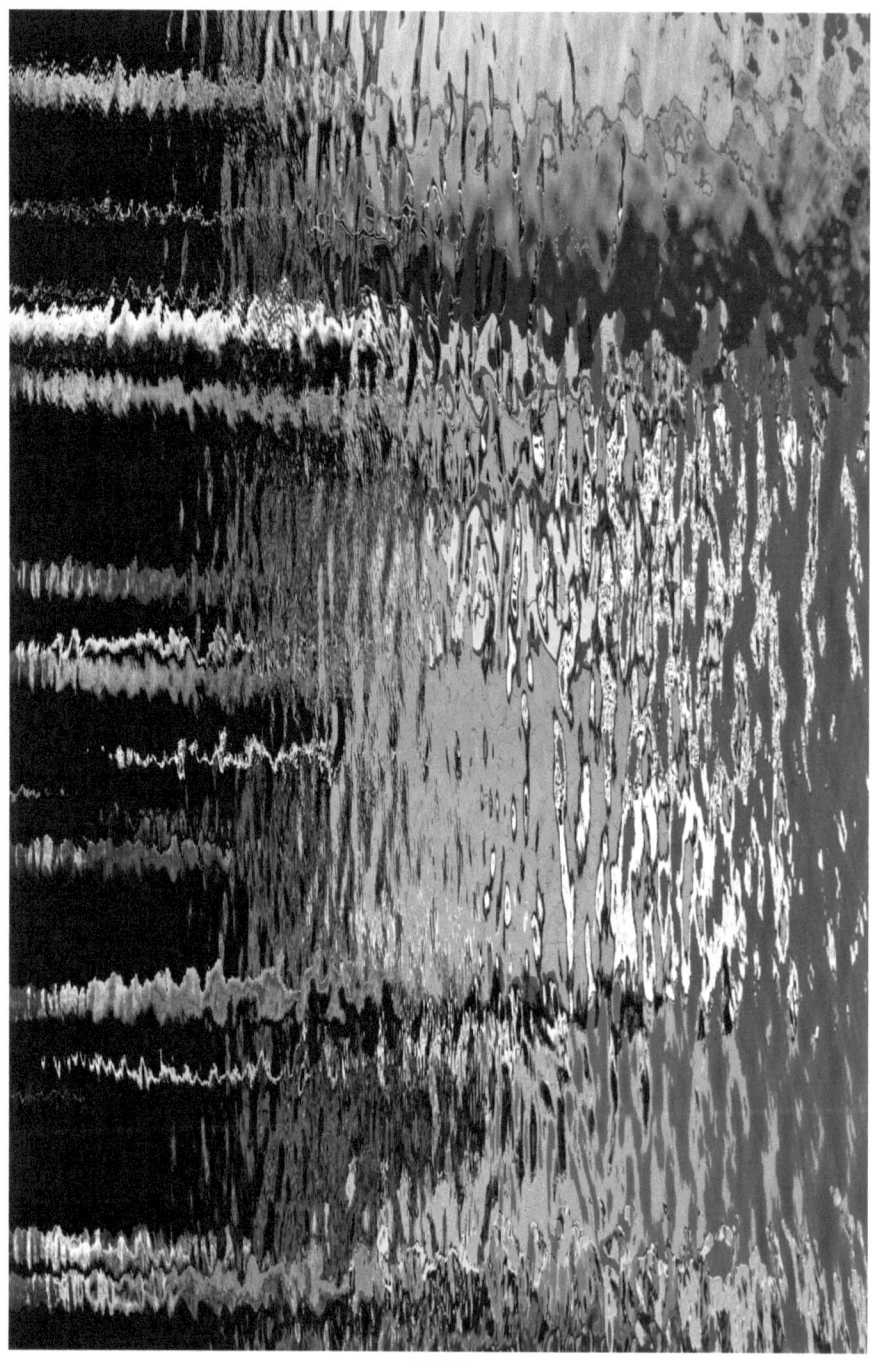

8766

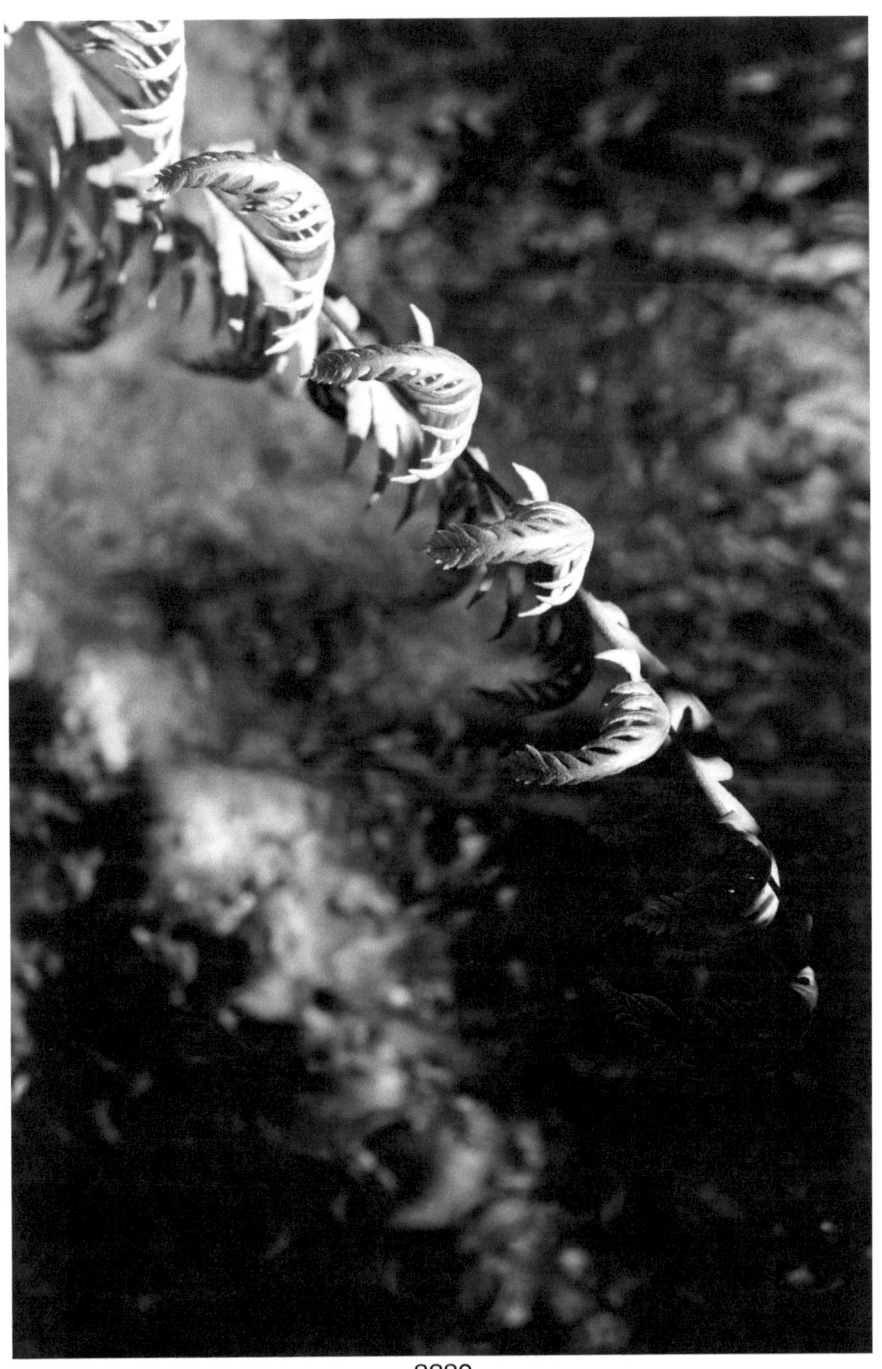

8889

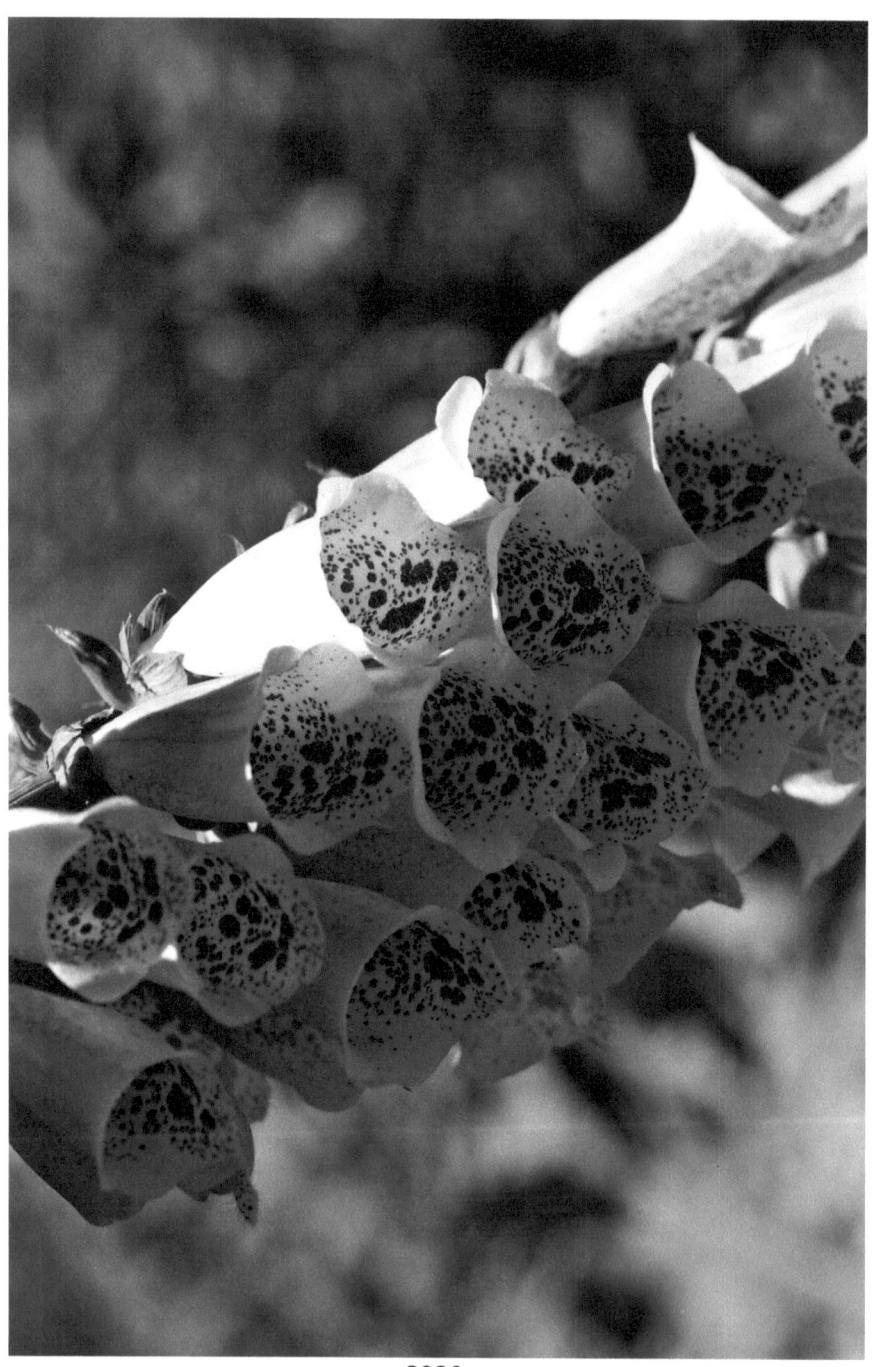

8920

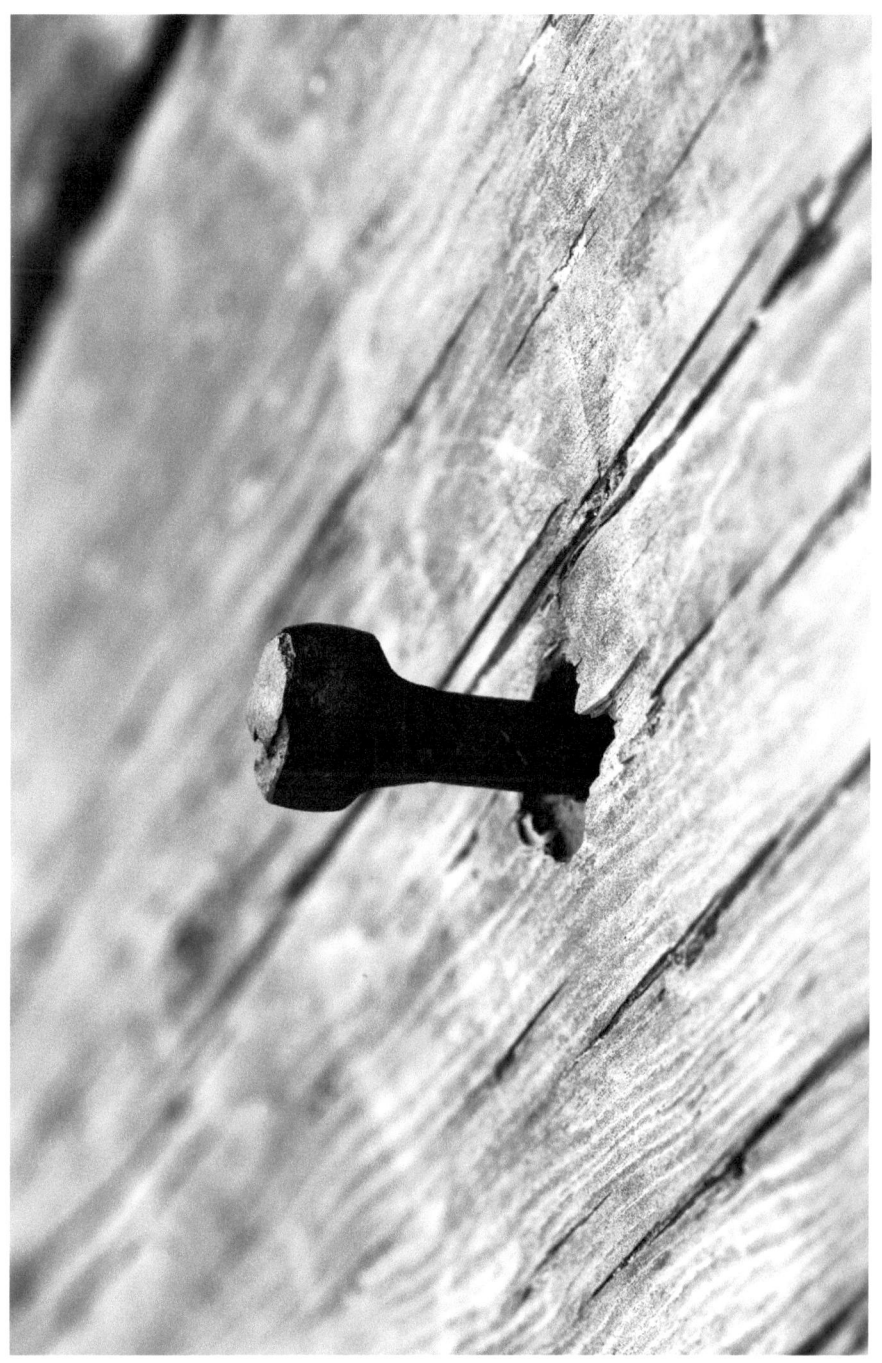

9024

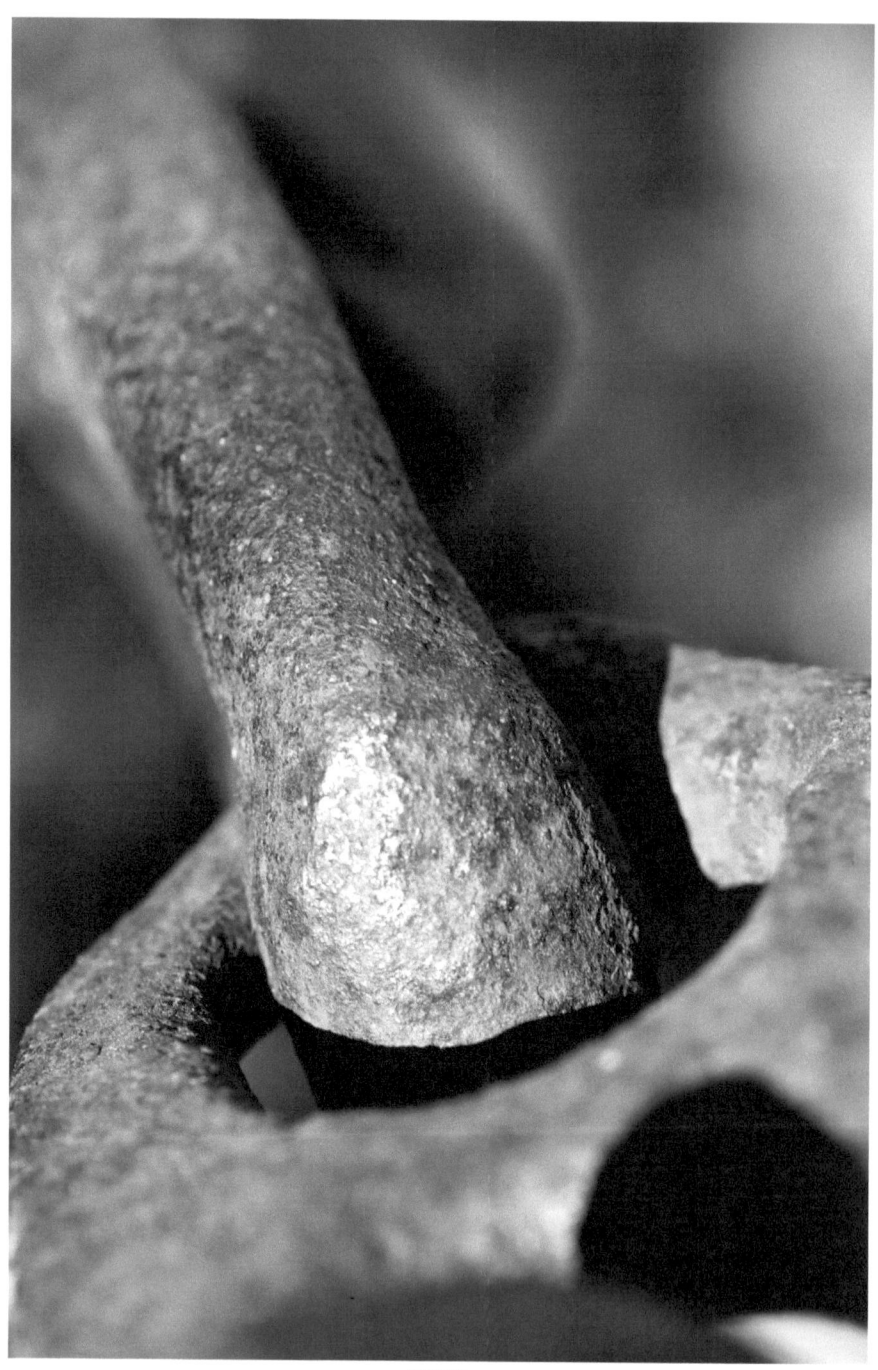

9353

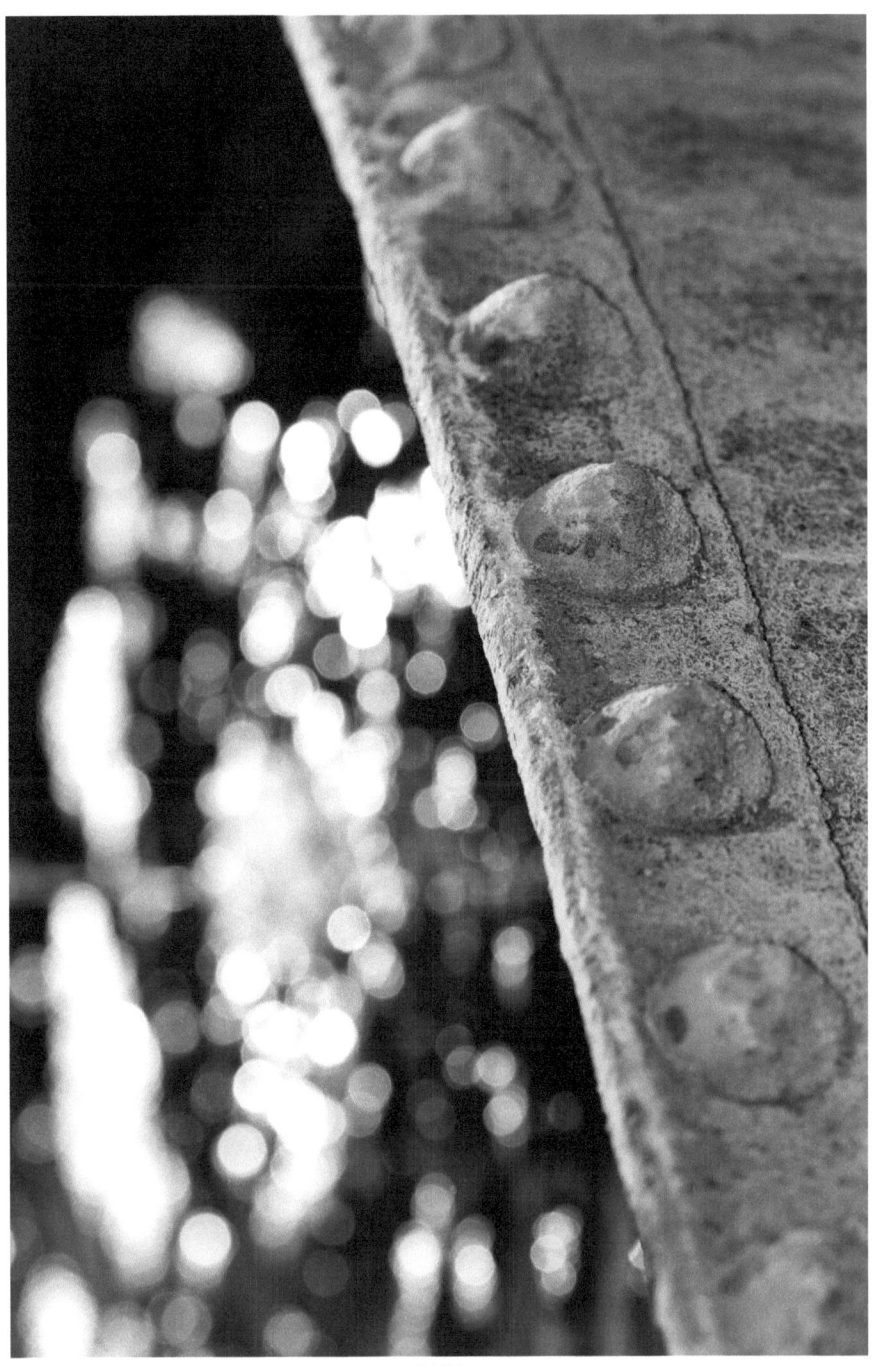

9430

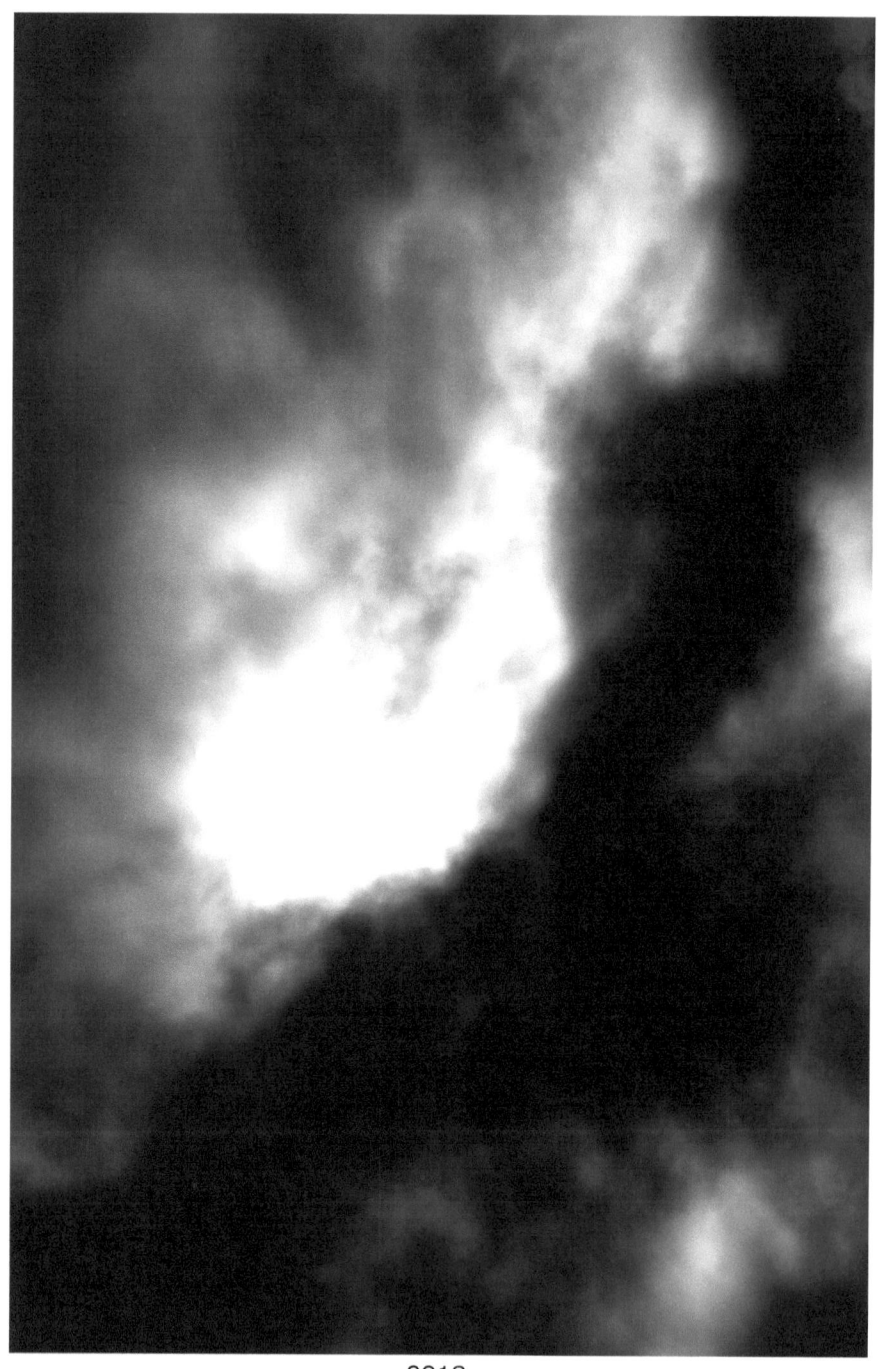

9918

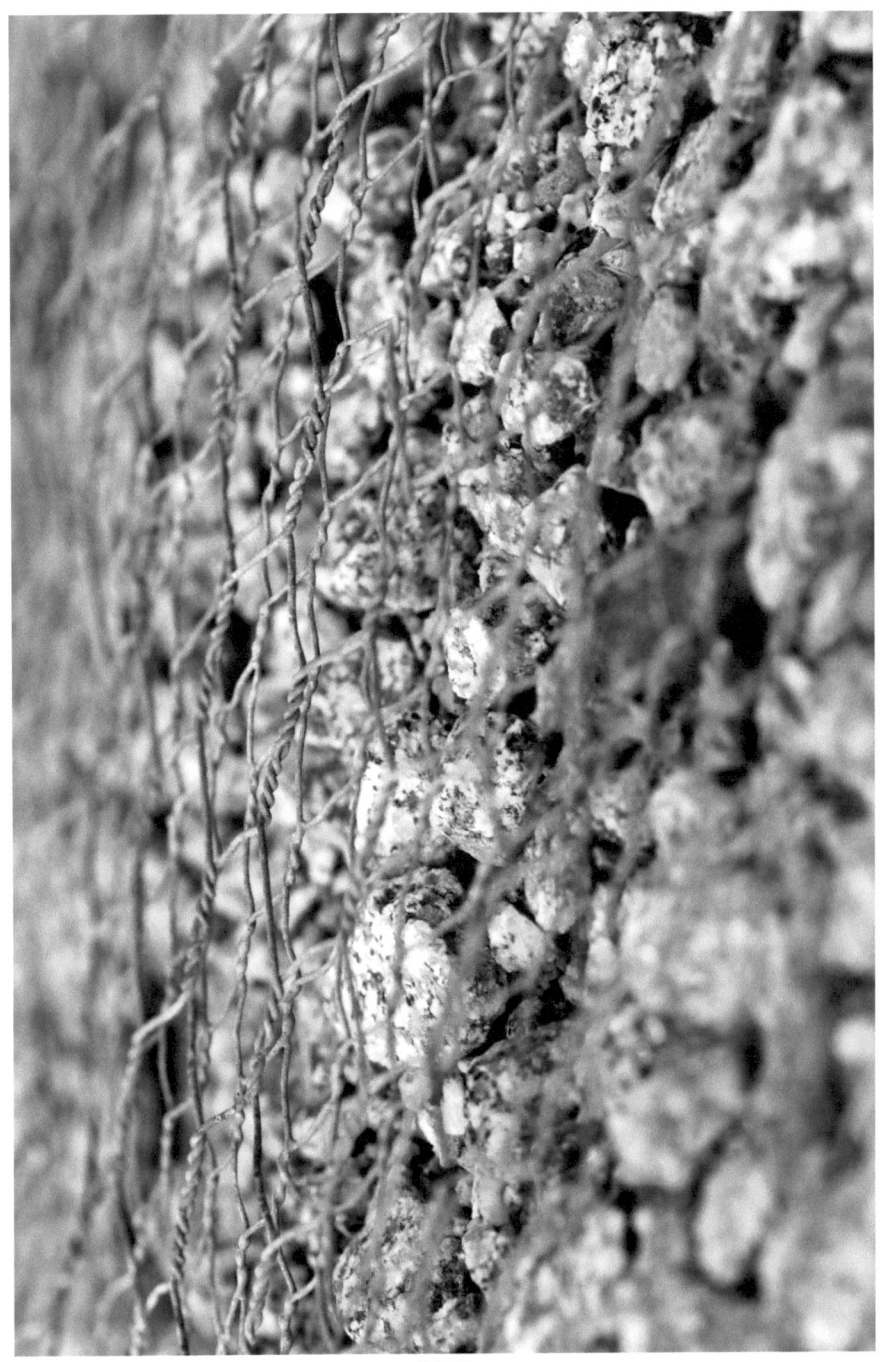

9970

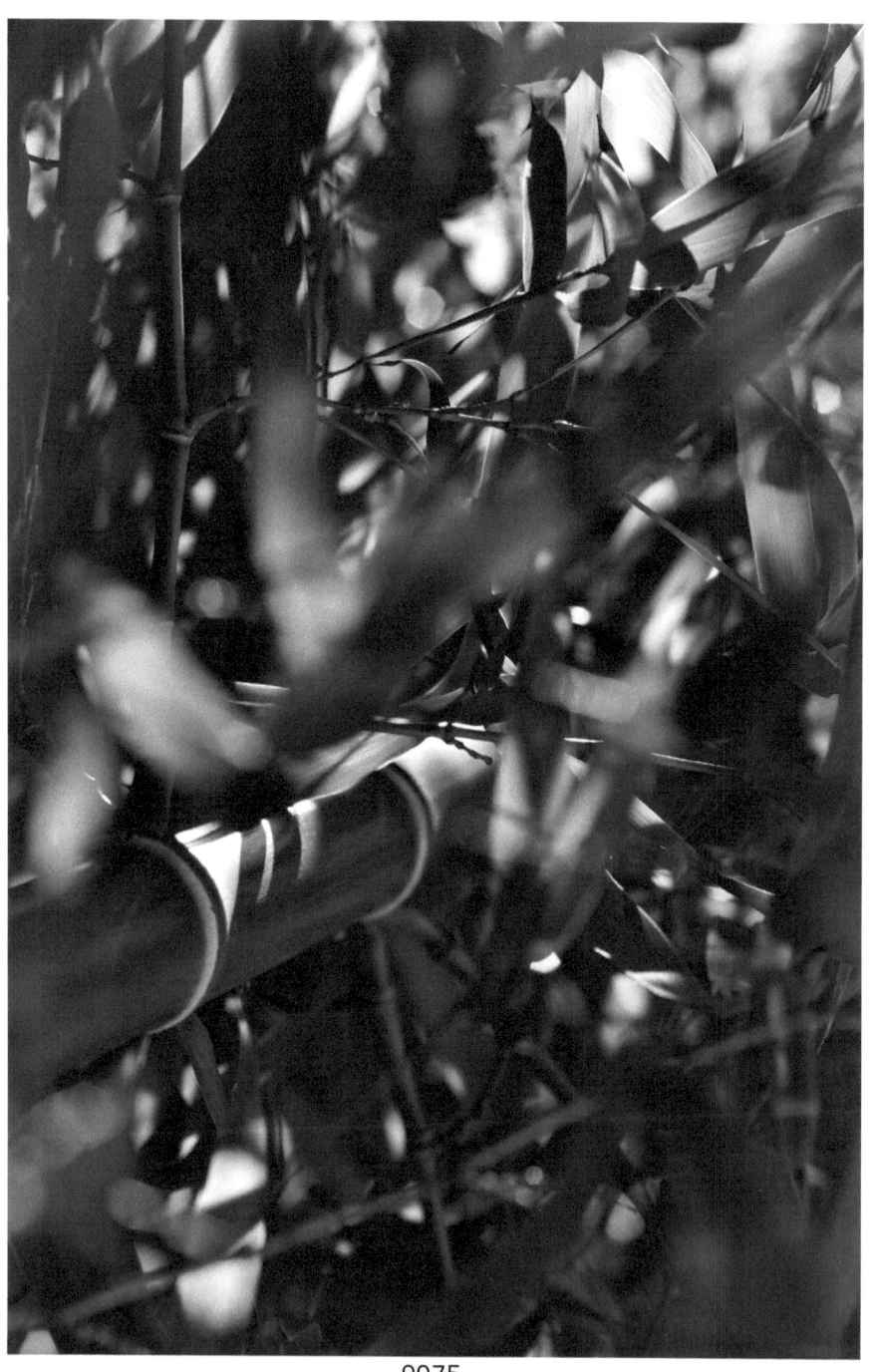

9975

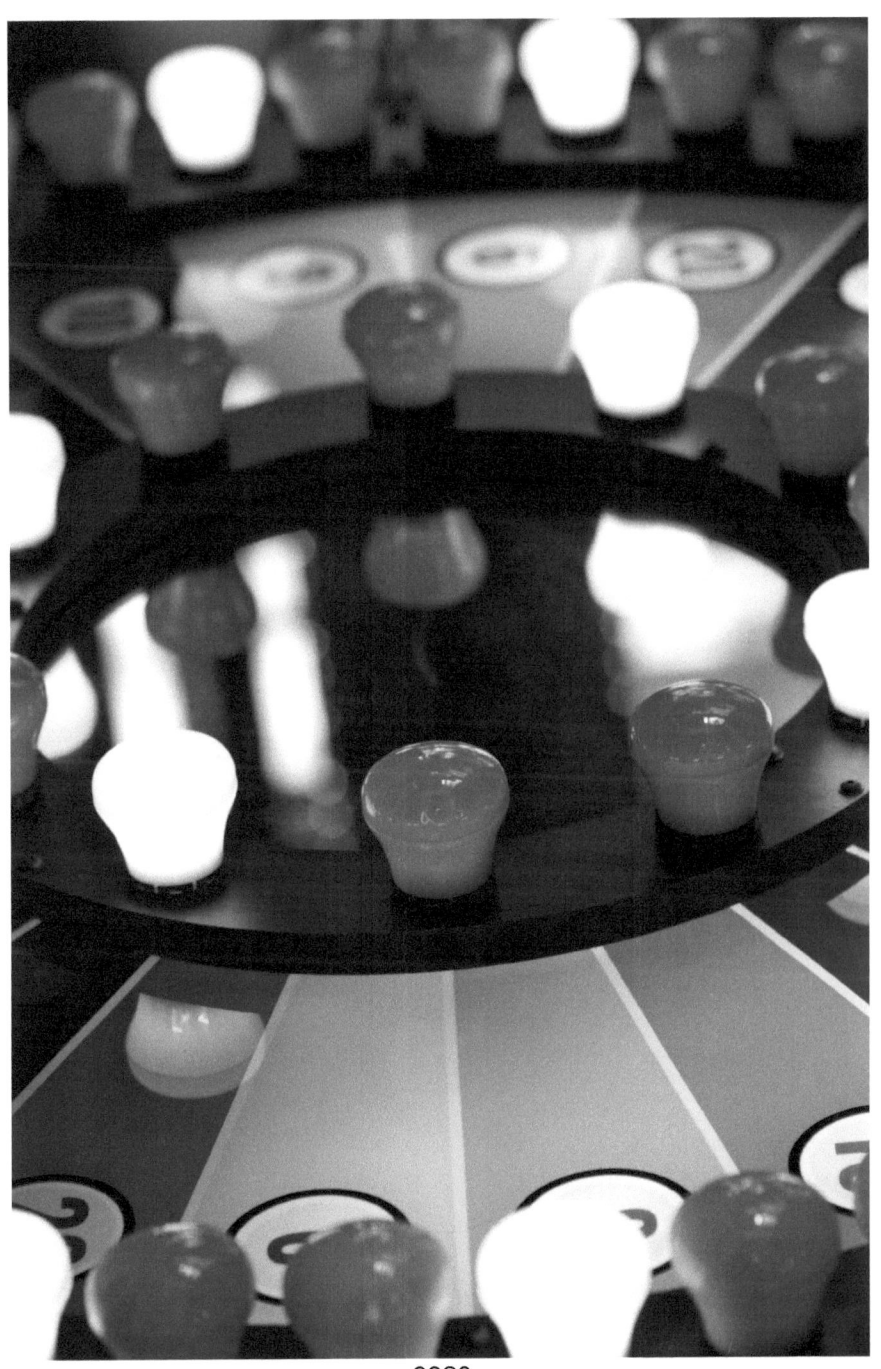

9980

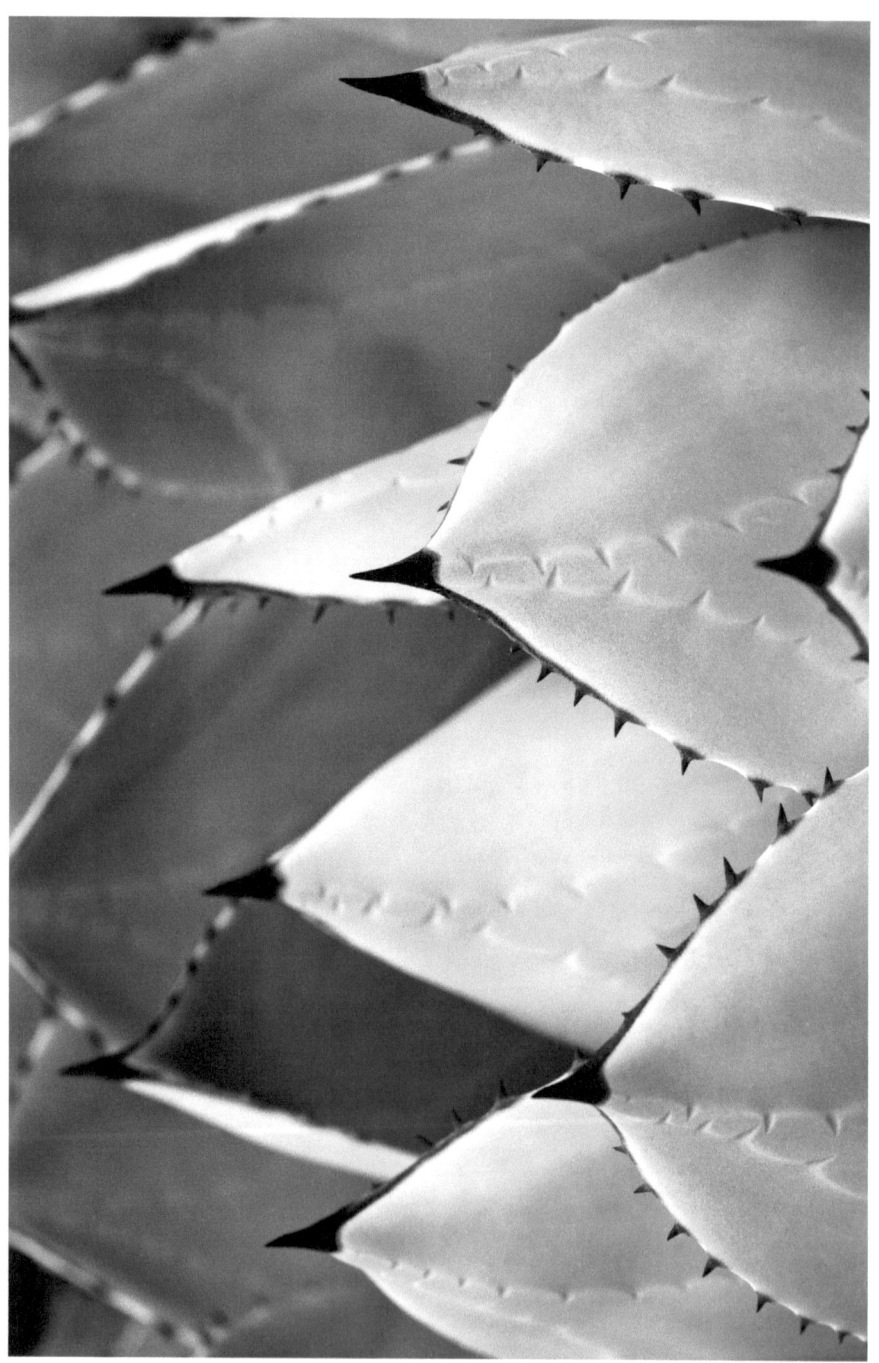

9993

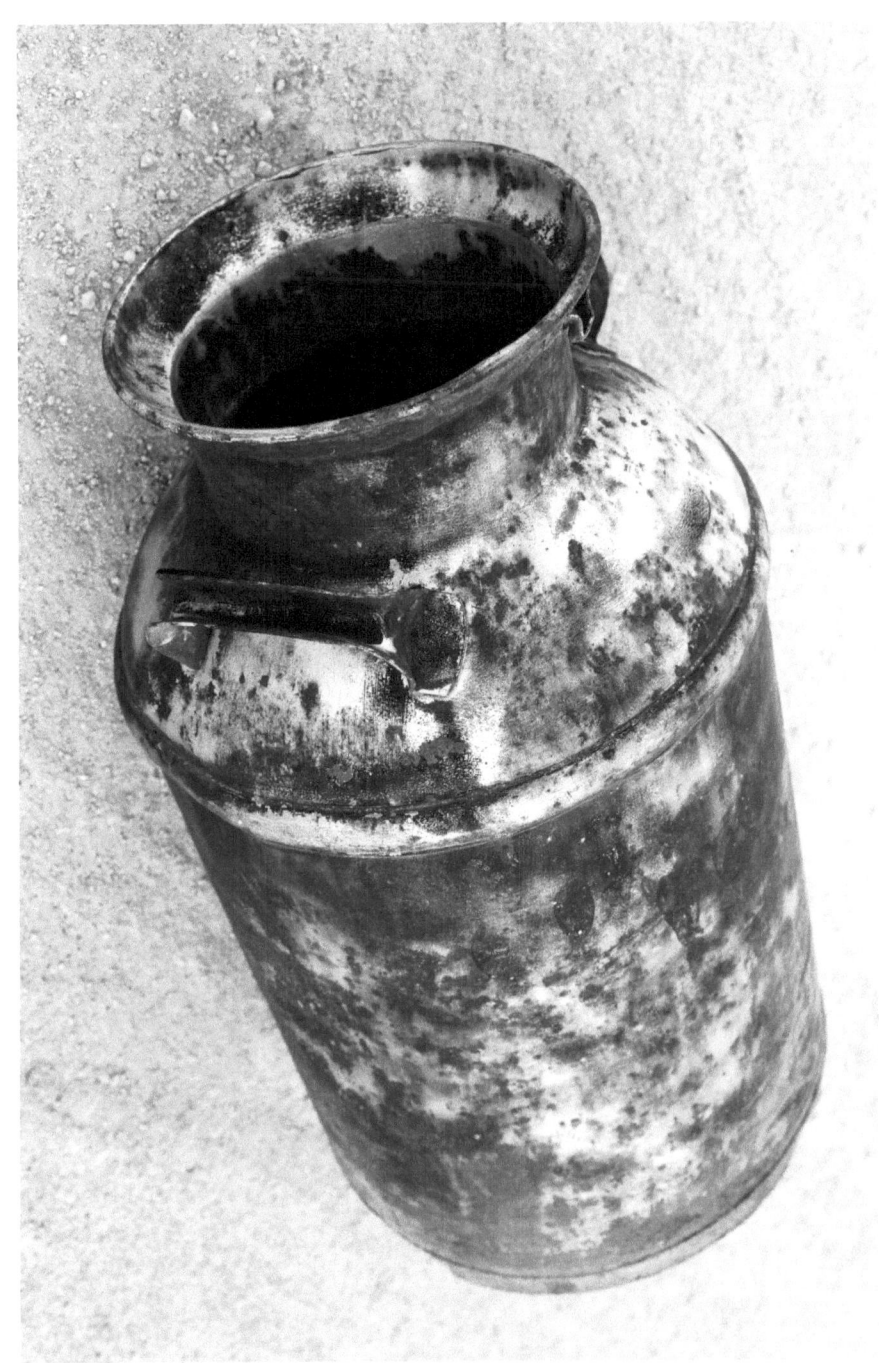

9994

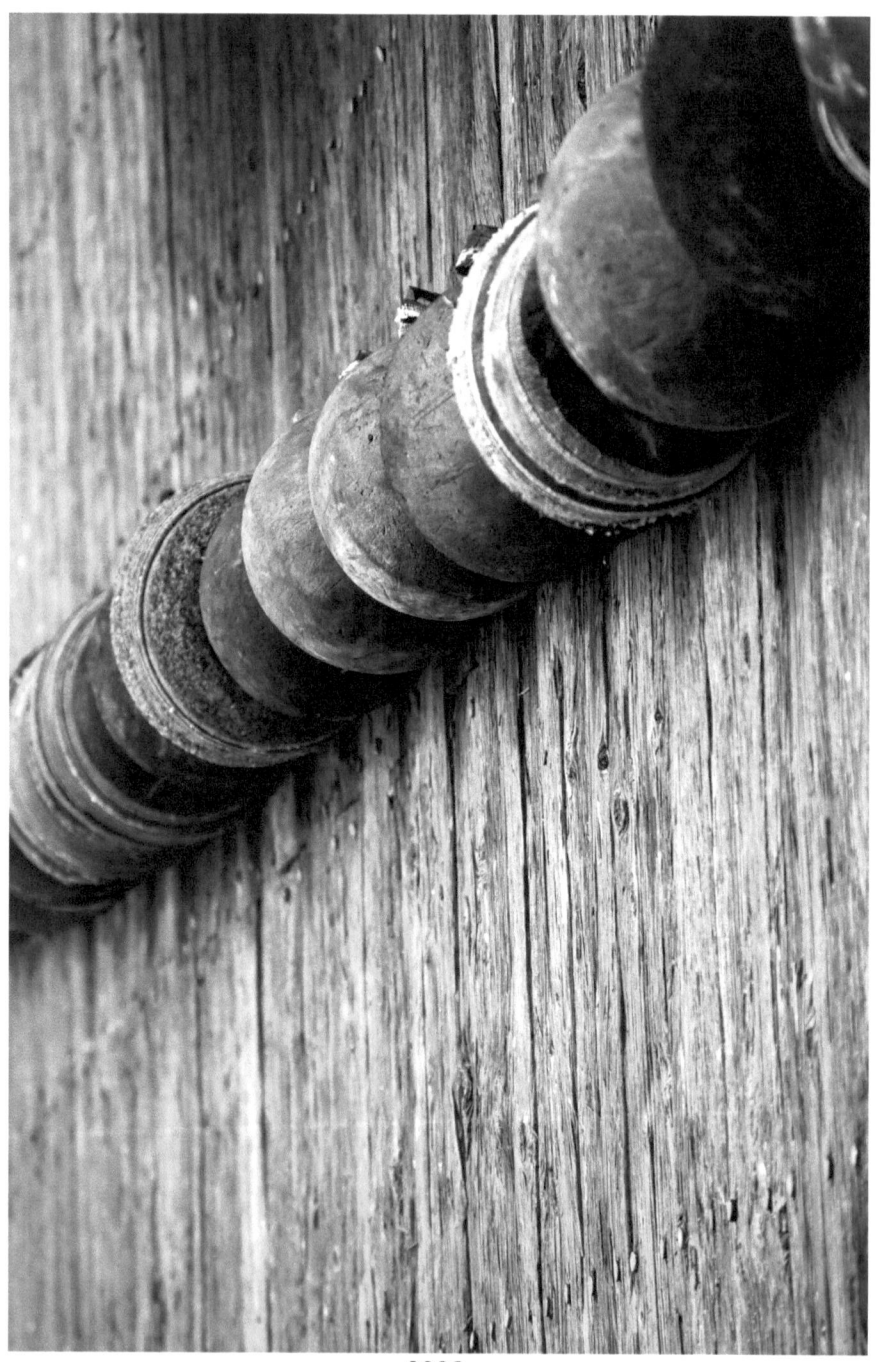

9998

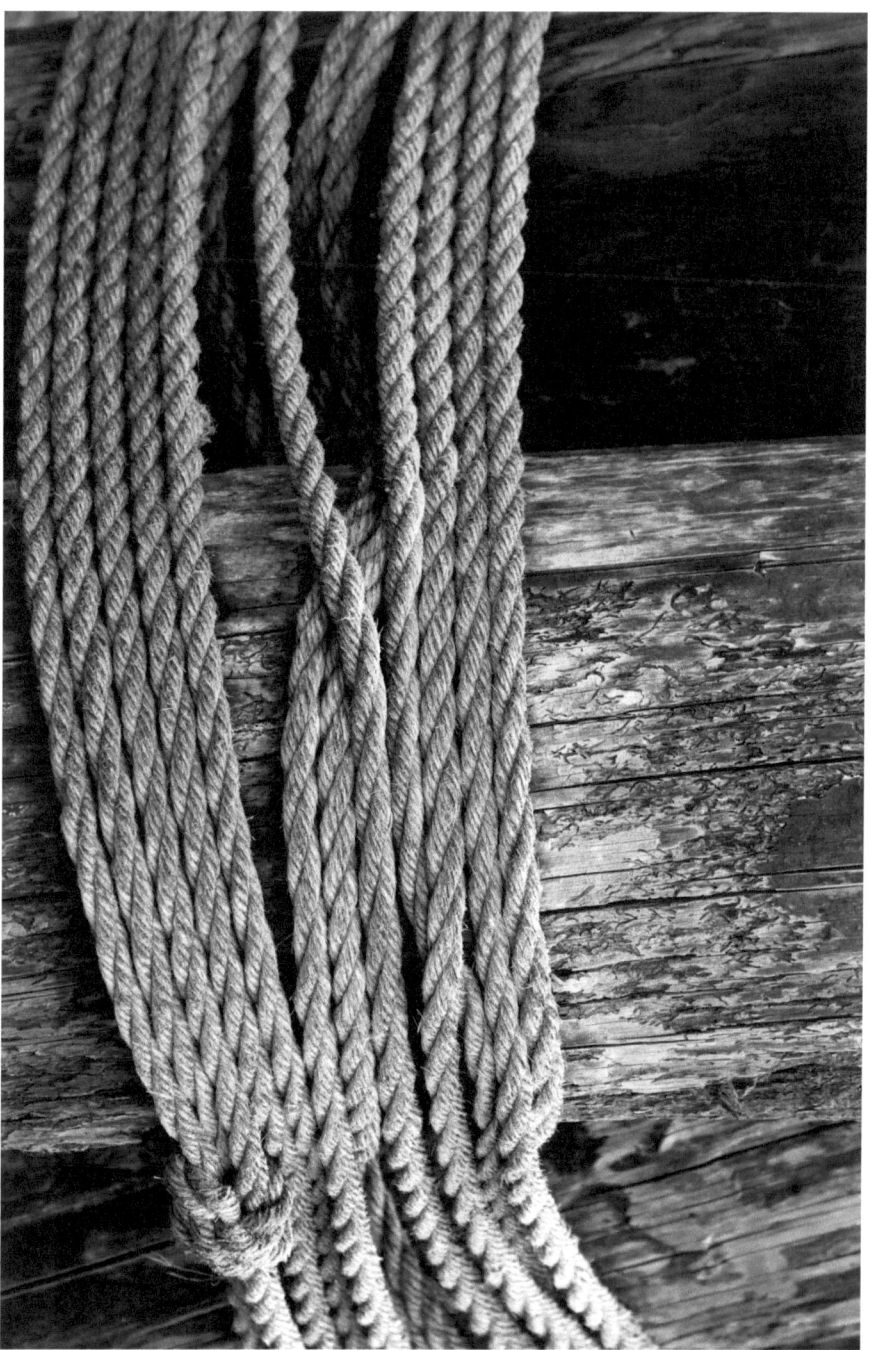

9999

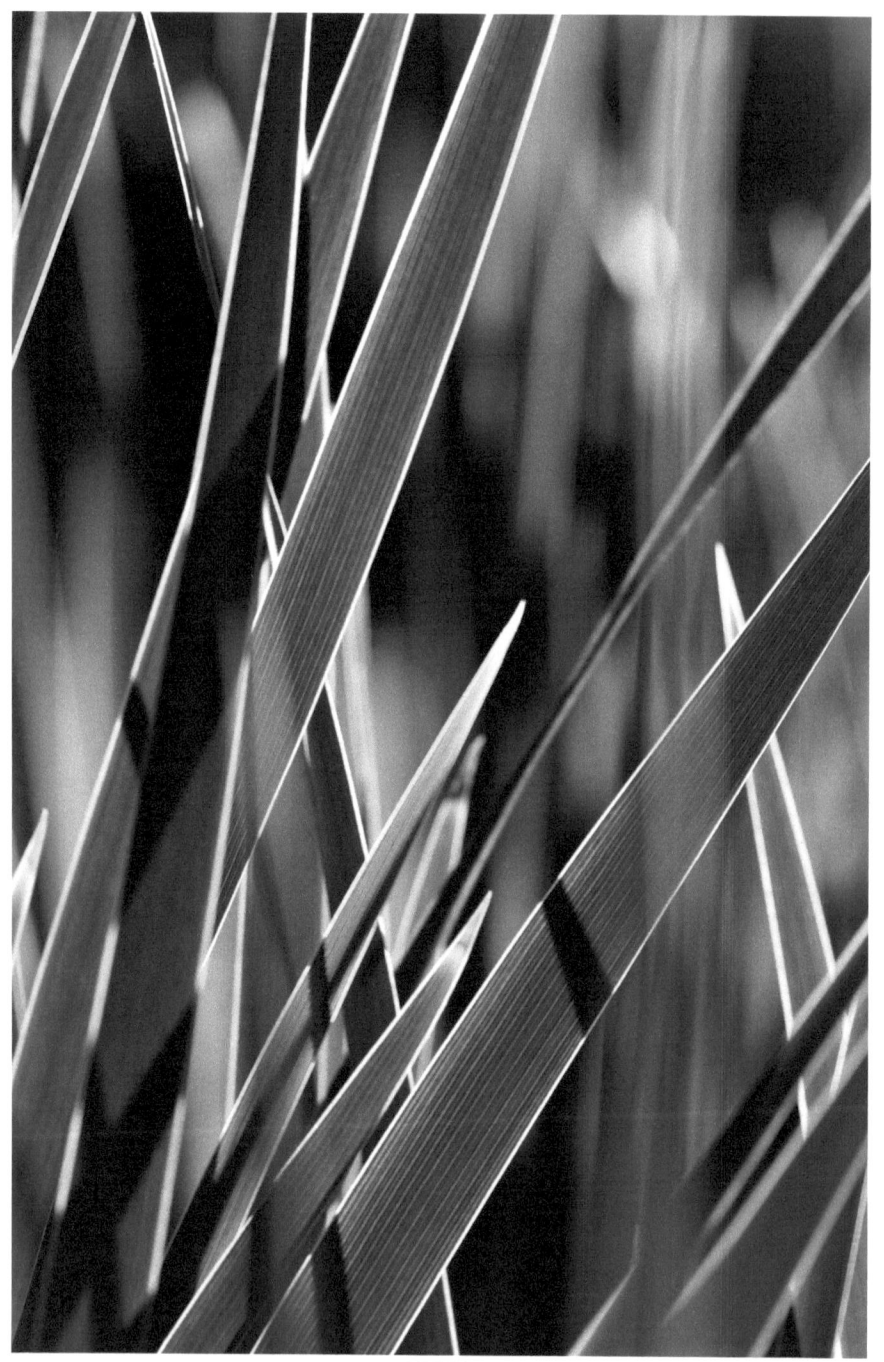

10000

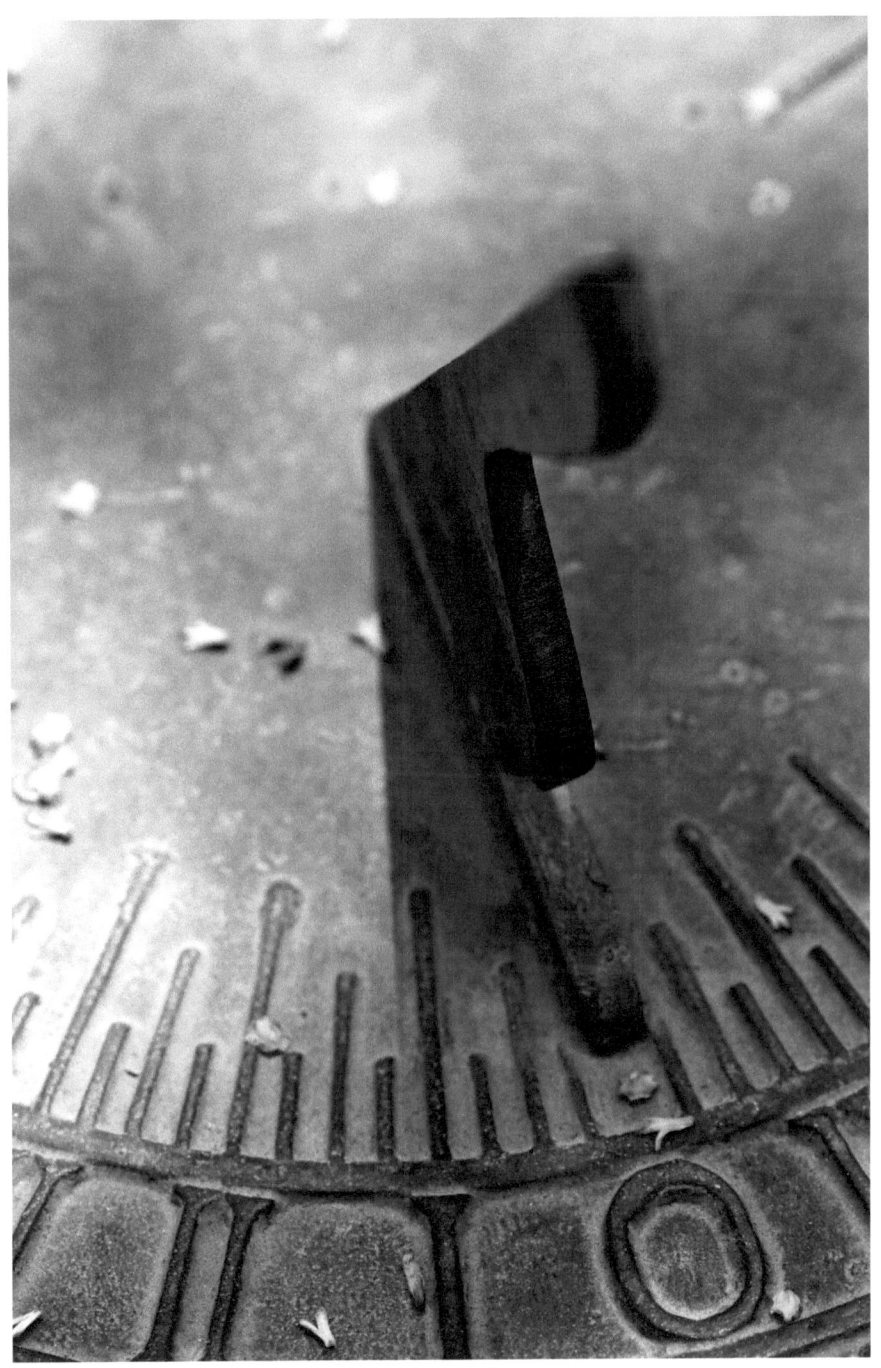

10002

www.ingramcontent.com/pod-product-compliance
Lightning Source LLC
Chambersburg PA
CBHW040840180526
45159CB00001B/259